The Nant Ffrancon pass.

Shire County Guide 33

GWYNEDD

Lawrence Garner

Shire Publications Ltd

CONTENTS

Printed in Great Britain by C. I. Thomas & Sons (Haverfordwest) Ltd, Press Buildings, Merlins Bridge, Haverfordwest, Dyfed SA61 1XF.

British Library Cataloguing in Publication Data: Garner, Lawrence. Gwynedd. — (Shire county guide, 33). 1. Gwynedd — Visitors' guides. I. Title. 914.29204859. ISBN 0-7478-0111-8.

NOTES
Cadw is the state authority responsible for the care of ancient monuments and historic buildings in Wales.

The locations of many of the places described in this book are identified by means of the national grid reference, given in the form of the two grid letters (denoting the 100 km square) and six figures, locating the site to within 100 metres. Each reference is preceded by the number of the Ordnance Survey (OS) Landranger map on which the place will be found: for example, OS 115: SH 818543. A full explanation of how to use grid references will be found on the Landranger maps.

ACKNOWLEDGEMENTS
Illustrations are acknowledged as follows: Caernarfon Air Museum, page 35 (top); CAT Machynlleth, page 50 (top); Gwynedd Archives and Museums Service, page 38; Cadbury Lamb, cover and pages 3, 5, 8, 11, 15, 20, 24-5, 36-7, 53, 55, 58, 59 (top), 60, 63 (top), 64, 66 and 69; Llanberis Lake Railway, page 46; Llechwedd Slate Caverns, page 35 (bottom); Museum of Childhood, Beaumaris, page 34; National Grid Company plc, page 68; Portmeirion Limited, page 49; Talyllyn Railway Company, page 47; Tudor Slate Works, page 50 (bottom). The remaining photographs are by the author.

Left: *Llanaber church, on the shore north of Barmouth.*

Cover: *View towards Harlech Castle.*

The Glaslyn estuary.

1
A view of Gwynedd

Some of the new counties produced by the local government reforms of 1974 were extremely controversial and continue to cause resentment to this day. The creation of 'Gwynedd' showed rather more imagination, because Gwynedd was the ancient kingdom of north-west Wales, and the amalgamation of the former counties of Anglesey, Caernarfonshire and Meirionnydd restored an historic unity.

A glance at the map will show that Gwynedd is a natural stronghold. Modern engineering has opened up easier communications, but until the nineteenth century access from the east by land was always hampered by the lack of river valleys that made other parts of Wales vulnerable; the only easy ways in were by sea, which severely limited the numbers of attackers, or along narrow and defensible coastal strips to the north and west. Invaders who achieved a foothold then had to contend with a natural fortress of complex mountain ranges, ideal for guerrilla warfare. It is hardly surprising that Gwynedd was the last major centre of Welsh independence.

The same intractable geography has dictated land use. Flat and fertile Anglesey has always been the food provider – *Mam Cymri*, the 'Mother of Wales' – and the island remains today a lowland farming area, hardly affected by the increasing holiday activity around its coasts. The same can be said of the Lleyn peninsula, although tourist development here is less intense and is largely confined to the Nefyn area on the north coast and Pwllheli in the south. The Lleyn interior is still a working landscape.

Most of the remainder of Gwynedd is contained within the Snowdonia National Park, a large area stretching from the north coast down to the Dyfi valley and taking in Bala at its most easterly point. This is the landscape that everybody associates with North Wales – spectacular mountain scenery, dramatic passes, tranquil lakes, grey towns and villages and pastoral river valleys hemmed in by hills.

The Park was designated in 1951, and certain areas considered 'ugly' were excluded, with the curious result that some places that are now magnets for visitors, such as Llanberis and Blaenau Ffestiniog, are outside the Park boundary. The Park authorities are fond of pointing out that it is not really a park at all, and it is useful to be reminded that this is a place where livings are earned and work goes on. Most of the land is privately owned and visitors are subject to all the usual restrictions on access, although there has long been an understanding that some well established mountain paths can be freely walked provided that no damage is done.

The mountain and valley landscape is the main attraction both to car-borne visitors and to walkers and climbers, and in the summer the main mountain roads can be uncomfortably crowded and parking virtually impossible. For this reason the bus service has been specially developed, and it is worthwhile obtaining details of services from tourist information centres (see chapter 14). The Sherpa service which runs on the roads in the Snowdon area is specially recommended for drivers who want to relax and enjoy the scenery.

There is, however, much more to Gwynedd than the mountains. In recent years the Forestry Commission has done much to open up its woodlands, and the forest trails, particularly in the forests of Coed-y-Brenin, Betws-y-coed and Beddgelert, can be very rewarding. The county abounds in fine sandy beaches, although Llandudno is the only sophisticated seaside resort. Others, like Nefyn, Criccieth and Barmouth, are pleasantly old-fashioned and ideal for family outings, and an increasing number of families seek out the small inlets and coves on Anglesey and Lleyn.

There is much to see, too, for those with special interests. The Edward I castles are unrivalled, there are some fine prehistoric sites, the industrial heritage has been imaginatively preserved and several narrow-gauge railways have been restored. History is the theme of most of the special tourist attractions that have emerged in recent years.

The aim of this book is to give a comprehensive picture of the choice of activities available in Gwynedd to visitors – a picture that is considerably more varied than the popular notion of caravan sites and strings of anoraked climbers.

The making of the landscape

It is often said that Snowdonia would once have rivalled the Himalayas, and certainly what we see now are the remains of mountains that have been worn away over millions of years. Some of Britain's oldest rocks are found here, formed by deposits on the sea bed when the whole area was at the bottom of the ocean 600 million years ago. These are the Cambrian rocks, created out of the erosion and decay of even earlier mountains. The undersea Cambrian 'mountains' decayed in their turn and other layers were deposited on top of them. This process, continued over an unimaginable period of time, has been divided by geologists into 'ages' with names like Ordovician, Silurian and Devonian.

The laying down of sedimentary deposits did not go on peacefully. At various times, and particularly during the formation of the second oldest rocks, the Ordovician, there was intense volcanic activity under the sea. This not only pushed up lava to form its own layers on top of the sediments but also forced molten rock into the sediments from below, thus producing areas of very hard 'igneous' rock. The whole mixture had varying degrees of resistance to erosion, and this helped to produce the peaks we see today.

Eventually came the point at which deep and massive movements within the earth forced the ocean bed above sea-level and the earliest North Wales landscape appeared. But this too became immediately subject to erosion, and the youngest and softest rock at the top of the heap – the Silurian – disappeared almost entirely. The harder Ordovician rock beneath was worn away in its turn until the huge mountains that must have existed were reduced to something like those we see today – dramatic, but the mere remains of huge masses and peaks. In addition to the forces of erosion, continued earth movements cracked the rock, overturned it and generally disrupted the strata to produce the present complex geology of Gwynedd. It is possible that the process included a period when Gwynedd was submerged once again, and that the Ordovician rock which predominates here was overlaid by much younger sediments which were too soft to survive when the earth surfaced again.

The last great influence on this landscape was the Pleistocene period, which began a mere million or so years ago. Usually known vaguely as the ice age, it involved the slow thawing and ponderous movement of huge ice masses, widening and smoothing out major valleys like Nant Ffrancon and scraping out giant cracks that were to become the steep valleys of small rivers. The ice also acted like sandpaper, smoothing off whole expanses of rock by the abrasive action of millions of stones carried within it. Other effects of ice movement were the litter of scattered boulders and scree in the mountain areas and the deposition of clay carried for considerable distances. (Shell Island, south of Harlech, is a famous example of this clay).

Looking at the geological map of Gwynedd,

we can see that the predominant rock is still the very old Ordovician with extensive areas of the even older Cambrian occurring extensively from Ffestiniog to Dolgellau – the Rhinog mountain range. Another notable Cambrian outcrop is Elidir Fawr, which has been quarried heavily at Bethesda and Llanberis for its high-quality slate, formed when fine rock sediment was compressed by the immense pressure of earth movements. Ordovician slate has been extracted on a large scale at Nantlle, north-west of Beddgelert, and at Blaenau Ffestiniog. The hard volcanic rock that produces granite occurs in a large area of Anglesey and is sprinkled throughout the rest of the county, notably around Dolgellau, where it has been used as the main building stone. Because of transport problems extraction of granite has been largely confined to coastal sites like Penmaenmawr and Trefor in the Lleyn peninsula, where it could be easily shipped. It is the volcanic rock that contains metals like copper, lead, gold and zinc, and mining has been a continuous activity in Gwynedd since Roman times – mostly on a small scale, although the copper-rich Parys Mountain in Anglesey is a spectacular exception.

Sygun Copper Mine, Beddgelert.

The early settlers

There are traces of human settlement in Wales dating from well before the final retreat of the ice in about 8000 BC, but it was the re-emergence of plant and animal life that produced the first appreciable numbers of mesolithic people, who lived a nomadic hunting life along the coastal strips, where their flint tools have been found. The first genuine settlers appeared in Britain in about 4000 BC, and it seems that western areas were among the first to be colonised, probably because the immigrants originated on the western coasts of Europe. They were people with considerable control over their environment, with the ability to grow food, domesticate animals and make boats, weapons, tools and pottery. They also traded, and among the more significant neolithic discoveries in Gwynedd have been 'axe factories' at Craig Llwyd above Penmaenmawr and on Mynydd Rhiw, near Aberdaron on the Lleyn peninsula. The large number of neolithic burial sites indicates that Anglesey and Gwynedd's western coast were quite heavily populated during this period.

While hunting for food was an essential feature of their lives, the evidence is that the neolithic people were comparatively sophisticated and peaceful, growing cereals and flax, rearing pigs and oxen and enjoying a well organised communal life that included religious practices. They had not discovered the use of metals, which first appeared with a wave of immigration into eastern and southern England in about 2500 BC, but over the next two hundred years signs of what is called the bronze age began to appear in Gwynedd. The most frequent evidence is a new form of burial – single interment in small round barrows rather than communal burial in long cairns (see chapter 3) – but the infiltration of bronze age people and customs does not seem to have affected the agricultural life.

There have been many discoveries of bronze tools, weapons and ornaments in Gwynedd, and their distribution shows that settlement was still largely confined to the coastal areas. But, as with neolithic axe manufacture, metal goods were produced in a few specific places and distributed by traders. The result is the series of ancient trackways through the mountains, particularly across the Rhinogs east of Harlech.

It was towards the end of the bronze age, perhaps around 1000 BC, that the first defensive structures began to appear on the land-

5

scape, although it is difficult to know whether the modest timber fences and earth ramparts were the result of communal strife or simply a way of establishing firm ownership of farmsteads. Almost certainly the fortifications marked the emergence of a political system that produced a ruling class based on well defined territories that had to be defended, but nobody knows how much serious warfare went on.

The rather vague picture of life in North Wales during the bronze age becomes clearer with the arrival of the Celts during the last one thousand years BC. Users of iron as well as bronze, they came originally from central Europe, and the migration to Britain was only a small part of a general Celtic expansion throughout Europe. As an aggressive people, socially well organised, artistic and technologically superior, they were able to exert a disproportionate influence, and by the first century BC they had imposed their language and their tribal way of life throughout Britain. The building of hillforts was intensified and communal farming expanded considerably, no longer in scattered independent farmsteads but in established centres, usually under the protection of a chieftain and in the vicinity of a hillfort.

The Druids fit somewhere into this picture, although their precise function has never been clear. They were apparently Celtic religious leaders and Anglesey was one of the great Druidic centres, particularly after the Roman invasion had forced Druids from the southeast of England to take refuge there. (They were to become a focus of opposition to the Romans for many years.) But whether it was a popular religion or the preserve of an exclusive group is not known. The Roman historian Tacitus is our main source of information, and he was no doubt writing from hearsay evidence, especially when he talked about the Druids' horrific human sacrifices. They probably had a monopoly of learning, which was passed on to students, but the absence of any written material preserves their mystery. Most modern 'knowledge' of them is accumulated romantic folklore.

In Gwynedd the Celtic tribe named by the Romans as the Ordovices was dominant, and their tightly knit society was in a position to put up a strong resistance to the Romans in the first century AD, although most of the major fighting was done nearer the present Welsh border. (Ordovicians were involved in the famous last battle of Caratacus.) The Romans never made a serious attempt to occupy Gwynedd, confining themselves to occasional punitive raids against guerrillas from their legionary base at Chester. Resistance virtually ceased after AD 78, and life among the Ordovicians seems to have gone on much as before.

The Romans were able to create a string of small forts linked by roads (see chapter 3) but never established a strong civil presence or real control. Certainly they were unable to coerce the Ordovicians into new towns, a policy followed successfully elsewhere. The numerous hut circles on Tre'r Ceiri in the Lleyn peninsula indicate an Ordovician settlement of considerable size, probably independent of any Roman rule, and Anglesey continued to be a Celtic outpost, with notable settlements at Din Lligwy and on Holyhead Mountain (see chapter 3). These are still visible, but there must have been many other sizable communities on the western side of the mountains and well away from Roman influence.

It followed that when the barbarian invaders forced the gradual withdrawal of the Romans from Britain Gwynedd was one area where Celtic culture had survived strongly, and this fact was to contribute greatly to future developments in religion and politics.

The age of the princes

The introduction to chapter 5 outlines the development of the Celtic Church. There is no doubt that the early conversion of the Celts in Gwynedd independently of Rome did much to promote a sense of unity from the sixth century onwards when the Celts were forced back into their mountain strongholds by successive waves of Anglo-Saxon settlers to the east. In Gwynedd there was pressure too from the Picts infiltrating from northern Britain, and from the Scots, who had long been attempting sea-borne raids from Ireland (the Roman fort at Holyhead had been created to combat them) and were now succeeding in getting a foothold.

The Celtic tradition of tribal chieftains continued, but the dangerous times encouraged larger groupings, and gradually a dynasty established itself in Gwynedd. There is a persistent tradition that a Celtic ruler called Cunedda came from southern Scotland with his eight sons in the fourth century to drive out the invaders from Ireland (bequeathing his name to the kingdom), and historians believe it possible that the Romans, desperately undermanned at the end, may have drafted in someone to relieve them of the task. We know little about these early kings, whose realm included Anglesey, Caernarfon and most of Meirionnydd. Maelgwyn, who died in the middle of the sixth century, claimed to be the great-grandson of Cunedda, and in the church at Llangadwaladr (see chapter 5) there is the grave slab of his successor, Cadfan, who died in AD 625.

The most famous of the early princes was Rhodri Mawr (AD 844-77), under whom Gwynedd became the dominant power controlling most of Wales, which by this time was isolated behind Offa's Dyke. His particular achievement was a successful campaign against the Danes, who had been fiercely attacking Anglesey and the western coast. Unfortunately Gwynedd lost its power rapidly after his death, subsiding in a flurry of conflict between minor chieftains, who ruled their small territories turbulently until after the Norman invasion.

William the Conqueror was not prepared to tolerate weakness on his western border, and he appointed experienced soldiers to earldoms in Hereford, Shrewsbury and Chester, with orders to subdue the Welsh. By 1075 Robert of Rhuddlan, deputy to the Earl of Chester, had advanced to the Conwy estuary and set up a castle at Deganwy. The Earl himself pushed on further, building the first castle at Caernarfon and establishing a Norman presence in Anglesey. By 1100, however, the chieftains of Gwynedd had fought back effectively, using the mountains to the best advantage and maintaining Welsh independence in the north-west when the rest of the country was subdued. They were even able to go on the offensive at times of crisis in England, for example during the chaos of Stephen's reign from 1135 to 1154.

Eventually Henry II was forced to come to terms, with an agreement that the Gwynedd princes would acknowledge him as king in return for autonomy in their own territories. As a result Gwynedd again became pre-eminent in Wales during the thirteenth century, under two notable rulers: Llewelyn ap Iorwerth (1194-1240) and Llewelyn ap Gruffudd (1247-82). They were not only powerful military leaders; they were careful to modernise the law and other institutions to strengthen their positions, and they copied the Norman example by building strategic castles (for example

Dolbadarn Castle, Llanberis.

at Dolbadarn and Castell y Bere) and by establishing boroughs like Caernarfon and Pwllheli as centres of trade. In 1267 Llewelyn ap Gruffudd was granted the title Prince of Wales by Henry III.

His success was short-lived. Edward I, who succeeded in 1272, decided to subdue Gwynedd once and for all, and after a brilliant campaign forced Llewelyn to sign away most of his power. To reinforce his supremacy Edward began a series of massive castles, including those at Caernarfon, Conwy, Beaumaris and Harlech (see chapter 4). Llewelyn had been allowed to keep his land in Gwynedd, but after yet another rebellion in 1282-3 Edward crushed further Welsh resistance and became undisputed king of Gwynedd, making his eldest son Prince of Wales. Later rebellions achieved some success, particularly that of Owain Glyndwr from 1400-15, but the advent of the Tudors restored order, and the Acts of Union of 1536 and 1543 merged Wales with England.

Farming and industry

The barren nature of much of mainland Gwynedd has always severely restricted the options for farmers. Until the sixteenth century subsistence farming based on sheep and some hardy types of cattle was the norm, but the growing demand for wool in the Tudor period encouraged the spread of extensive sheep farming. The use of available land was maximised by the custom of allowing the sheep to graze the mountain tops in the summer while the better lowland grazing was reserved for winter use, and this system is still widely used, together with the modern practice of wintering stock on lowland farms. For most mainland farmers there will never be a real alternative to sheep.

Wool, however, has become a sideline, and the main saleable product these days is sheep meat, particularly the famous Welsh lamb. The distinctive breed of sheep seen all over the county, long-legged and agile, is not impressive to look at but is one of the hardiest. Visitors often wonder why the flocks, left to themselves for long periods on the mountains, do not get irretrievably lost, but the successive generations of ewes carry an ancestral memory of their territory and straying is a minor problem; for this reason it is impossible to import a new flock into the mountains.

In recent years the hardy beef cattle breed known as the Welsh Black has grown in popularity throughout Britain, and it is not uncommon now to see these cattle grazing at high altitudes in the areas where they were first developed.

Fertile Anglesey has always been a special case. From very early times it was the granary of North Wales, and its exports of corn across the Menai Strait were an essential part of its economy, as well as being a life-sustaining factor for the mainland. Modern farming economics have virtually put an end to large-scale cereal production, and modern road transport has enabled the good-quality grassland to be used for dairying, an activity that has also increased on the Lleyn peninsula.

Early industry in Gwynedd was based heavily on wool production, especially in the eastern part of the county. The cloth produced from Welsh sheep was never of the highest quality, but there was a substantial demand in the eighteenth and nineteenth centuries for flannel (significantly the only Welsh word that has been generally adopted in English). Towns tended to specialise: Bala, for example, was noted for its knitted hose. It is still possible to see wool production going on, partly as a tourist attraction, but the industry has ceased to be significant.

Mining has been a recurrent activity since Roman times, because Gwynedd is rich in a variety of metals such as copper, gold, silver, manganese and lead. However, apart from a copper boom on Anglesey during the eighteenth and early nineteenth centuries, there has never been a consistently successful mining industry, largely owing to the remoteness of the sites and transport problems.

The industry which has most clearly left its mark on the county is quarrying. The phenomenal demand for roofing slate as towns and cities in England expanded during the nineteenth century brought prosperity to many areas, and especially to the large slate centres at Bethesda, Llanberis, Nantlle and Blaenau Ffestiniog. The hard igneous rock granite was also exploited for roadstone in coastal places like Penmaenmawr and Trefor, where the heavy product could be easily shipped away. Quarrying still continues on a minor scale.

It would be wrong to ignore the effect of the tourist industry on Gwynedd, which has given rise to much heart-searching, but there is no doubt that the decline of traditional industries would have caused much hardship without the active encouragement of holiday activity.

Haymaking at Beddgelert.

The shore of the Mawddach estuary near Barmouth.

2
Coast and countryside

BEACHES

The main seaside resorts are noted in chapter 12, but Gwynedd has a wide choice of other good beaches, the majority of them to be found on Anglesey and the Lleyn peninsula. Those mentioned below are all reasonably accessible by car and suitable for family outings.

Anglesey

Beaches are described anti-clockwise round the island.

Traeth Bychan. This is a small and sheltered sandy cove about 1¹/₂ miles (2 km) south of Moelfre, with a car park at its northern end.

Traeth Lligwy. This large and popular beach north-west of Moelfre has car parks reached either from Moelfre or by turning off the A5025 at Brynrefail. It is possible to walk to the adjacent beach of Traeth-yr-Ora, which is otherwise not readily accessible.

Cemaes Bay. Cemaes is an attractive small harbour. Its sandy beach lies to the east and has its own car park, which can be reached from the A5025 without entering the rather cramped village.

Porth Swtan (Church Bay). This pleasant small beach on the north-western side of the island is flanked by rocks. There are refreshment facilities and a car park at the end of a minor road signposted off the A5025.

Porth Trwyn. This is a secluded bay, but parking is not easy.

Porth Trefadog. A good beach with limited parking, this can be quite quickly reached by walking from Porth Tywyn-mawr.

Porth Tywyn-mawr. This large sandy beach is popular, but seldom uncomfortably crowded, and has good parking facilities.

Trearddur. This miniature resort on the western side of Holy Island is quite unsophisticated and has useful facilities. The intricate rocky coastline has several small sandy bays and there is a large beach at Trearddur itself.

Rhoscolyn. Lanes from here lead to Borthwen and Silver Bay, both quiet and unspoilt and with interesting rocks.

Rhosneigr. This large holiday village has broad sandy beaches on each side. The village can be avoided by using the car park off the A4080, 2 miles (3 km) north-west of Aberffraw.

Porth Trecastell. This is a good sheltered beach, but the easy access just off the A4080 leads to crowding in the summer.

Newborough. A road from the village runs through a forest to a car park near the Llanwddyn sands. There is plenty of room here, and the chance of an interesting walk to Llanwddyn Island.

Lleyn peninsula
Dinas Dinlle. At the extreme north-eastern end of the peninsula, just south of Caernarfon, this beach is best reached by turning off the A499 through Llandwrog.

Trefor. There is a convenient car park for this rather shingly beach, which lies beneath old granite quarries.

Traeth Penllech. 6 miles (10 km) south-west of Nefyn, this is a long stretch of sand and seldom crowded because of its comparative remoteness and the distance from the car park to the beach - about ½ mile (800 metres) of walking.

Porth Iago. This tiny secluded cove is reached by a succession of minor roads off the B4413. There is a private car park owned by Ty-mawr Farm.

Porth Oer. A mile (1.6 km) south of Porth Iago, these are the famous Whistling Sands. There is a car park and a quite steep descent to the beach.

Porth Neigwl (Hell's Mouth). This 4 mile (6 km) stretch of sand, largely inaccessible, has a reputation for being dangerous for swimmers. It is best reached at its extreme eastern end by way of Llanengan.

Porth Ceiriad. Lying between Porth Neigwl and Abersoch, this is a very pleasant sandy beach. The Ordnance Survey map will be useful to find the car parks at Nant-y-big Farm

(SH 308251) and Pant Farm (SH 314254).

The western coast
Apart from the beaches at Criccieth, Barmouth and Tywyn the following are worth investigating.

Black Rock Sands. A little to the east of Criccieth, these extensive sands are best reached from Porthmadog through Morfa Bychan.

Llandanwg. Reached by a turning off the A496 south of Harlech, this is a pleasant beach noted for its half-buried church. There is a car park and there are some shops in the village. Bathing is safer at the northern end of the beach near the church.

Dyffryn Ardudwy. This is 6 miles (10 km) south of Harlech. A turning off the A496 south of the village leads to a car park above the beach.

COASTAL WALKING
Gwynedd holds plenty of opportunities for fine coastal walks. Footpaths are shown on the Ordnance Survey map, but the following are particularly recommended.

Anglesey
From Bull Bay (north-west of Amlwch) to Cemaes. This is a fine stretch of cliffs with three headlands owned by the National Trust.

Cemlyn Bay. 2½ miles (4 km) west of Cemaes.

Porth Swtan to Porth Trwyn. This good shorter walk begins 2½ miles (4 km) south of Carmel Head.

Holy Island. Between South Stack and North Stack.

Lleyn peninsula
From Porth Dinllaen to Porth Widlin. Porth Dinllaen (see under Porthmadog in chapter 12) lies beneath a headland from which it is possible to walk westwards for over 10 miles (16 km) along the cliffs.

From Braich y Pwll to Aberdaron. Braich y Pwll (National Trust) is the westernmost point of the Lleyn peninsula. For Aberdaron see chapter 12.

Llyn Trawsfynydd.

From Porth Ysgo to Rhiw. This stretch of coastline is owned by the National Trust. Access is from Ysgo (OS 123: SH 207267).

COUNTRY PARKS

The Great Orme, Llandudno.

Although this headland has been an extension of the holiday resort for over a hundred years it can still be a rewarding place to visit. Access from the town is by footpath, cable car or tramway to the summit, where there are refreshment facilities and a visitor centre (no telephone), which gives information about history and wildlife. Although the summit area becomes crowded in summer it is possible to find unfrequented paths all round the headland, offering the chance to see traces of prehistoric life as well as a wide range of seabirds and the herd of feral goats. The Great Orme is a limestone outcrop, so fossils abound.

Llyn Padarn, Llanberis. Visitor centre at the Quarry Hospital, Y Gilfach Ddu, Llanberis. Telephone: 0286 870892.

The lake, overlooked by the impressive Dinorwic quarries, is very attractive, and a walk around it is one of the main features of the Park. Other leaflets describe shorter walks in the old quarry area, and there is also a lakeside railway. (See chapter 7 for The Power of Wales and the Welsh Slate Museum and chapter 9 for the railway.)

CYCLING ROUTES

At the time of writing Gwynedd County Council is planning a series of cycle tracks, and it would be worth inquiring about these at information centres, which also supply details of cycle hire firms. The first track to be opened is the Lon Eifion route, which uses a former railway line stretching from Caernarfon to Bryncir, north of Criccieth.

FOREST TRAILS

In recent years the Forestry Commission has opened up many of its forests to visitors. The facilities range from simple parking space to picnic sites and toilets, but in each case there are waymarked walks. Enthusiasts for this type of walking should first visit the visitor centre at Maesgwm (see Coed-y-Brenin, below), where leaflets and maps for the whole county are available – do not rely on finding copies in the boxes at the sites. Alternatively most local tourist information centres have details. The following are major sites.

11

Beddgelert Forest

Waymarked walks start from the Glan y Gors car park (OS 115: SH 575500). Maps and information are available at the Beddgelert tourist information centre (see chapter 14).

Cae'n-y-coed Arboretum (OS 115: SH 768574); signposted off A5, 2$\frac{1}{2}$ miles (4 km) west of Betws-y-coed.

The waymarked walk passes through an arboretum containing over one hundred species of trees.

Coed-y-Brenin Forest. Visitor Centre at Maesgwm, off A470, 8 miles (13 km) north of Dolgellau.

The centre has displays providing an introduction to the forest and it is possible to obtain a map and leaflets describing a number of waymarked trails, including the Rhaeadr Mawddach and Pistyll Cain waterfalls.

Dyfi Forest

There are three main starting points for walks: the car park and picnic site off the A487, 2$\frac{1}{2}$ miles (4 km) south of Corris (OS 124: SH 759054), the picnic site at Foel Friog, 1 mile (1.6 km) north-east of Corris (OS 124: SH 769093) and from the Talyllyn Railway station at Abergynolwyn (OS 124: SH 671064).

Gwydir Forest

Betws-y-coed lies at the centre of this forest area, and the National Park information centre at The Stables gives full information about the many walking opportunities.

Llanystumdwy. 2 miles, (3 km) west of Criccieth.

The Llwyber Coed Trefan walk leads from the Lloyd George Memorial (OS 123: SH 475386) through woods alongside the river Dwyfor. There is another waymarked forest walk from the nearby car park at SH 461386.

Newborough Forest, Anglesey.

A minor road from Newborough (OS 114: SH 424656) leads to a car park beside the sand dunes of Newborough Warren. Various paths start here, although equally attractive is the walk across to nearby Llanddwyn Island.

NATURE RESERVES AND TRAILS

The remote countryside of Gwynedd has encouraged the establishment of many nature reserves, some of them with restricted access.

Visitors particularly interested in exploring them should contact the Nature Conservancy Council (NCC) for information, guides and permits where necessary. Alternatively, the Penmaenpool Nature Information Centre at the southern end of the Mawddach tollbridge, west of Dolgellau (OS 114: SH 695185) will supply a wide range of information. The following are a few of the more popular and accessible sites.

Aber Falls. Off A55, 7 miles (11 km) east of Bangor. There is a parking place at Bont Newydd (OS 115: SH 662720).

A 2 mile (3 km) walk up the Afon Goch valley leads through oak woods to the dramatic waterfall known as Rhaeadr Fawr. A NCC leaflet describes this walk and a return path which together comprise the Coedydd Aber Trail.

Cemlyn Bay, Anglesey. 2$\frac{1}{2}$ miles (4 km) west along the coast from Cemaes.

The shingle bay holds a lagoon which is a haven for seabirds. The path along the top of the shingle bank is closed from April to June.

Cwm Idwal Trail

Cwm Idwal is an early and very famous reserve. The trail starts at Ogwen Cottage (OS 115: SH 649604) and in its circuit of Llyn Idwal takes in the typical high mountain scenery of the Glyders and the Idwal Slabs (appropriate clothes and footwear needed). Most of the plant habitats are around the lake, where cinquefoil, butterwort, quillwort, lobelia and awlwort flourish. Birds to be seen here include ravens, choughs and wheatears. The NCC pamphlet is essential to get the most out of this trail.

Cwm Nantcol. Reached by a minor road off A496 at Llanbedr, south of Harlech, with parking at OS 124: SH 607272.

The main natural features are the Nantcol gorge and waterfalls. (The interesting chapel near the car park is the starting point for a farm trail.)

Malltraeth

In the early nineteenth century it was decided to reclaim the extensive marshland to the north-east of Malltraeth, on the southern coast of Anglesey. A causeway was built across the head of the estuary and the river Cefni was channelled into a canal. It is poss-

The Bird Rock in the Dysynni valley.

ible to walk for several miles beside the canal to observe the wildfowl in the marshes. On the south side of the A4080 just to the east of the village is a pool that has become an official reserve, with a range of wading birds. Redshank can be seen here in the late spring.

Morfa Mawddach walk

This is not a formal reserve but a good nature walk along the Mawddach estuary, starting at the Nature Information Centre, Penmaenpool (OS 124: SH 695184) and following the track of an old railway line. The estuary water and marshland provide excellent opportunities for birdwatching.

Penrhos, Holyhead.

Off A5 on the eastern outskirts of Holyhead, the former Penrhos estate is now dominated by an aluminium smelting works, but 450 acres (182 ha) of the land are taken up by a reserve that provides both woodland and sea environments for a wide variety of birds.

South Stack

At the westernmost point of Holy Island, 3 miles (5 km) west of Holyhead, is the South Stack lighthouse. On the cliffs to the northwest of it is a Royal Society for the Protection of Birds reserve with viewing facilities to enable visitors to study the shags, cormorants, razorbills, fulmars and other seabirds. Ellin's Tower, near the lighthouse, is an RSPB visitor centre.

OTHER OUTDOOR EXCURSIONS
Afon Lliw to Afon Gain mountain road

The road leaves the A470 south of Trawsfynydd (OS 124: SH 710349), climbs to the Gain valley, passes through a forest plantation and crosses deserted moorland before dropping to Llanuwchllyn along the Lliw valley. At Llanuwchllyn there is a chance to board the Bala Lake Railway (see chapter 9) for a lakeside trip to Bala.

Beddgelert: Welsh Highland Railway track

This railway once ran through to Porthmadog, where a short stretch is being restored. At Beddgelert the trackbed is a right of way and provides a fine walk southwards through the Aberglaslyn pass to Nantmor (OS 115: SH 600460). As its name implies, Aberglaslyn once stood at the mouth of the river Glaslyn and could be reached by ships, but the sea was cut off in the early nineteenth century by the embankment at Porthmadog (see Porthmadog in chapter 12).

13

Cregennen lakes. National Trust.

On the opposite side of the Mawddach estuary from Barmouth, Arthog is the starting point for an enjoyable walk to these lakes. The path starts by the church (OS 124: SH 647146) and passes waterfalls in the woodland before emerging into open country. Other walks lead from the lakes.

Croesor

A steep lane leaves the B4410 above Tan-y-Bwlch (OS 114: SH 616416) to reach Croesor, where a car park marks the start of a fine valley walk.

Cwm Pennant

This lovely valley is reached by taking a minor road off the A487 at Dolbenmaen, 12 miles (19 km) south of Caernarfon (OS 115; SH 507432), and provides a safe but splendid walk among remote mountains.

Dysynni valley

This valley, running into the hills from Bryn-crug, north-east of Tywyn (OS 135: SH 609034), is full of interest. 4 miles (6 km) from Bryn-crug the road skirts Craig yr Aderyn (Bird Rock), a remarkable crag that is a nesting place for cormorants. 2 miles (3 km) further on are the splendidly sited remains of Castell y Bere (see chapter 4), and just beyond is the village of Llanfihangel-y-pennant, with a small medieval church, but best known as the home of Mary Jones. In 1800, at the age of sixteen, she walked almost 30 miles (49 km) barefoot over the mountains to Bala to obtain a Bible from Thomas Charles, the Methodist minister. The event is reputed to have inspired him to found the British and Foreign Bible Society. Mary's ruined cottage can still be seen.

Llanddwyn Island, Anglesey.

The island is actually a long thin promontory with rocky cliffs and small sandy coves, reached from the car park at Newborough Warren (OS 114: SH 406634). It first became famous as the sanctuary of St Dwynwen, patron saint of lovers, whose shrine here became an object of pilgrimage. More recently it carried a pilot station, a lifeboat and a lighthouse, all now disused. There are the ruins of a sixteenth-century church and a row of tiny cottages once used by the pilots and lighthouse keepers. One of them has been restored to its original condition and another is a visitor centre. Since the island is part of the Newborough Warren nature reserve it is necessary to keep to the established paths.

Llyn Alaw, Anglesey.

This is a very large reservoir with a visitor centre (OS 114: SH 373856) reached by turning off the B5109 west of Llangefni. The lake is rich in trout, and the centre issues fishing permits. The water also attracts wildfowl, and observation facilities have been set up on the eastern side of the lake at SH 404866. The church of Llanbabo, near the visitor centre, is of great interest.

Mynydd Bodafon, Anglesey.

This rocky outcrop, 3 miles (5 km) west of Moelfre, provides a short but mildly energetic walk with magnificent views on a clear day. A lay-by at OS 114: SH 476855 is the start of a track and path to the summit, from which Snowdonia and much of Anglesey are visible.

Segontium Roman fort near Caernarfon.

3
Sites of archaeological interest

Although there is evidence of human activity in Wales perhaps 250,000 years ago, the first substantial signs of prehistoric settlement in Gwynedd date from after 3000 BC and take the form of neolithic chamber tombs, designed for communal burial. Archaeologists distinguish between various types of chamber tombs and passage graves, but the common features in each are a burial chamber (sometimes with side chambers) constructed with vertical walls topped by a capstone, some form of entrance passage reinforced with stones and a covering either of stones or earth. In most cases the covering has disappeared over centuries of exposure, leaving the supported capstone standing alone. Several of these passage graves have survived in the county, including two particularly fine examples described below. Gwynedd is also dotted with the small round cairns characteristic of the bronze age, when communal burial gave way to individual interment, but such survivals are usually insignificant to look at and often go unrecognised, so they are not included here.

Other characteristic landscape features dating from the later neolithic and the bronze age (roughly 2500 to 1600 BC) are standing stones and stone circles, the purpose of which is still debated. The circles probably had a ritual purpose, and it has been suggested that they may have been a means of astrological calculation, but excavation has shown that some were also sites for burials.

Celtic remains, dating from the period 500 BC to AD 400, include several hillforts. (The word 'hillforts' is misleading because it is now recognised that many were used for different purposes at different times, but no better term has been devised.) Many of these sites date from the later bronze age and were developed more elaborately by the Celts. None of the Gwynedd forts is particularly complex, but their situations alone justify a visit. The county is fortunate in having substantial remains of two extensive Celtic settlements occupied well into the Roman period, both of them well preserved.

As might be expected, the Romans left few traces because their presence was spasmodic and always military, as they never established a permanent civil community, but there are surviving remains of three forts, and one of

15

*The Bodowyr burial chamber,
Brynsiencyn, Anglesey.*

them, *Segontium*, has now been thoroughly investigated and the findings have been made available to the public by means of a visitor centre.

Archaeological enthusiasts will consult the specialist gazetteers; the sites listed below are those likely to be rewarding for the non-specialist visitor, and they are all freely accessible unless otherwise stated.

Enquiries about all sites in the care of Cadw, the Welsh Historic Monuments Commission, should be made to the Marketing Officer, telephone 0222 465511.

Barclodiad-y-Gawres, Aberffraw, Anglesey. OS 114: SH 328708. Off A4080, 2 miles (3 km) north-west of Aberffraw. Cadw.

In a cliff-top position overlooking Porth Trecastell, this is one of two exceptional neolithic passage graves in Anglesey, dating from 3000 to 2500 BC. It appears to have consisted originally of an earth and stone cairn about 90 feet (27 metres) in diameter, with a 20 foot (6 metre) passage of dry-stone construction leading to the main tomb chamber, which had three side chambers leading off it. The remarkable feature of the tomb is the decoration on three slabs to left and right of the entrance to the chamber. Slabs at the back of the side cham-

bers also carry patterns, making this an important example of prehistoric art. This evidence has led archaeologists to connect Barclodiad-y-Gawres with similar tombs in Spain, Portugal and Ireland. Excavations in 1952 revealed fragments of burnt human bone and a hearth with an assortment of animal bones. One of the side chambers contained traces of a funeral urn, indicating that the grave had been reused later in the early bronze age.

In view of the importance of the site a concrete cover was placed over the tomb after the excavations. The tomb is normally locked, but the key is available either from Beaumaris Castle or at the Wayside Cafe in Llanfaelog, the village 1 mile (1.6 km) to the north. A torch is essential.

Bodowyr burial chamber, Brynsiencyn, Anglesey. OS 114: SH 462681. 2 miles (3 km) north-west of Brynsiencyn. Cadw.

This is another neolithic passage grave, but in the form in which most of them have survived – a large capstone supported on upright stones.

Bryn Celli Ddu, Brynsiencyn, Anglesey. OS 114: SH 506702. Off A4080 2 ½ miles (4 km) north-east of Brynsiencyn. Key normally at the farmhouse. Cadw.

This passage grave ranks with Barclodiad-y-Gawres in importance. It has been established that the circular site incorporates two successive structures, a stone circle or 'henge' replaced by a chamber tomb. The henge was encircled by a ditch 17 feet (52 metres) wide, 6 feet (1.8 metres) deep and about 70 feet (21 metres) in circumference (a section remains on view). The fourteen stones, of which only two remain, were set within the ditch, and burnt bones at the foot of one of them indicate that the henge was associated with burials. It is believed that the circle was broken up when the chamber tomb was constructed.

The tomb has a chamber about 8 feet (2.4 metres) in diameter and 6 feet (1.8 metres) high, reached by a passage 27 feet (8.2 metres) long. The covering cairn was originally about 80 feet (24 metres) in circumference, larger than the restored version, and its base was set on stones embedded in the original henge ditch. The two upright slabs at the door would have carried a capstone to form an entrance to the passage, which has a bench on the right-hand side. Within the chamber is a single upright stone. Just beyond the chamber, at the centre of the original stone circle, excavators found a human bone in a pit which had been covered by an elaborately patterned slab (this is in the National Museum of Wales and has been replaced by a cast). The pattern is similar to others found in Spain, and the evidence is that the new burial chamber might have been the work of recent immigrants.

Caer Gybi Roman fort, Holyhead. OS 114: SH 248826. Cadw.

The parish church of St Cybi stands within the walls of a Roman fort built in the late third or early fourth century AD as a defence against the increasing attacks by barbarian coastal raiders. It has been suggested that one function of the fort may have been as the shore base for scouting ships. Substantial remains of the walls survive, roughly 10 feet (3 metres) high and 5 feet (1.5 metres) thick, and there are the remains of defensive towers at the corners.

Caer-y-Twr, Holyhead. OS 114: SH 218830. On the summit of Holyhead Mountain, reached by a path from the car park at South Stack. Cadw.

This is a very simple hillfort, probably built in a single phase, and using a dry-stone wall to supplement natural crags. The wall still stands 10 feet (3 metres) high on the northern side. The Ty Mawr hut circles nearby, which may well have been occupied in Roman times by the descendants of the fort builders, are described below.

Canovium Roman fort, Caerhun. OS 115: SH 776703. 5 miles (8 km) south of Conwy off B5106.

The remains, dating from late in the first century AD but probably rebuilt in the second, are slight but their situation is extremely attractive. The fort appears to have guarded the river crossing of the Chester-Caernarfon road. A medieval church now occupies part of the site.

Capel Garmon burial chamber, Betws-y-coed. OS 115: SH 818543. At Capel Garmon, 2 miles (3 km) east of Betws-y-coed. Cadw.

The tomb chamber was enclosed by a long cairn, of a type found in the Cotswolds. It had an elaborate false entrance at its east end, but the real entrance was on the south side, and a passage leads from here into a rectangular antechamber with a tomb chamber on each side, one of which has its capstone in position.

Castell Bryn Gwyn, Brynsiencyn, Anglesey. OS 114: SH 464671.

This is a defensive site, possibly adapted as late as the first century AD from a much earlier henge monument (neolithic pottery and other remains have been found).

Cefn Coch stone circle (The 'Druids' Circle'), Penmaenmawr. OS 115: SH 723746. 1 mile (1.6 km) south of Penmaenmawr by public footpath.

The circle is situated about half a mile (0.8 km) to the east of what is known to have been a major neolithic axe factory. Out of the original thirty stones ten survive. (For this and other archaeological sites in the neighbourhood see the 'History Trail' available in Penmaenmawr.)

Creigiau Gwineu, Rhiw, Lleyn peninsula. OS 123: SH 228274. On National Trust land reached by a path south-west of Rhiw.

Apart from a length of stone wall and at least one hut circle, there are few remains of the fort on this craggy hill, but the expedition is recommended for the exceptional views.

17

The Dyffryn Ardudwy burial chambers.

Din Lligwy hut group, Llanallgo, Anglesey. OS 114: SH 497861. 1 mile (1.6 km) north of Llanallgo. Cadw.

This very fine site contains the foundations of a group of huts, possibly of iron age origin but adapted and occupied during the Roman period. It has been suggested that the two circular and seven rectangular huts represent a chieftain's farmstead. The site is surrounded by a thick boundary wall.

Dyffryn Ardudwy burial chambers, Barmouth. OS 124: SH 589229. By the school in Dyffryn Ardudwy, on A496, 5 miles (8 km) north of Barmouth. Cadw.

A single collapsed cairn evidently covered two distinct tombs 30 yards (27 metres) apart. The smaller one, on the western side, has three uprights and a capstone, but the stones of the later chamber have tumbled. At this and similar sites there is little doubt that the original massive cairns were used as a convenient source of stone for field walls and early farm buildings.

Llech Idris, Trawsfynydd. OS 124: SH 731311. 3 miles (5 km) up the lane leaving A470 on the southern outskirts of Trawsfynydd.

This is one of the more accessible and dramatic standing stones, 11 feet (3.4 metres) high and situated close to a mountain track developed by the Romans and probably much earlier in origin.

Lligwy burial chamber, Llanallgo, Anglesey. OS 114: SH 501861. ½ mile (0.8 km) north of Llanallgo. Cadw.

A massive capstone estimated to weigh nearly 30 tons is supported on three out of the original eight wall stones. A natural cleft in the rock was used to form the tomb chamber here. The Din Lligwy hut group is nearby (see above).

Moel Goedog, Harlech. OS 124: SH 614325. Off a mountain track leading from the minor road between Llanfair and Eisingrug.

There are several traces of prehistoric life here. Moel Goedog itself is a small, double-

18

ramparted fort. Beside the track to the south-west are two burial chambers, and a short distance to the south-east, beside another track, are signs of huts and Celtic field boundaries. The Ordnance Survey Outdoor Leisure map shows very clearly the ancient track leading away over the mountains to the north-east – a very rewarding walk on a fine day.

Pen-y-Gaer hillfort, Llanbedr-y-Cennin. OS 115: SH 750693. 6 miles (10 km) south of Conwy off B5106.

Standing at 1200 feet (366 metres) above sea-level, this is a fort with a double rampart, triple in places, notable for its rare *chevaux de frise* defences – pointed stones laid upright in the ground to deter soft-shod attackers. There are traces of hut circles.

Plas Newydd burial chamber, Llanfairpwll. OS 114: SH 521697. In the grounds of Plas Newydd (see chapter 6). Charge for entry to house and grounds.

There is no covering cairn here, but the burial chamber is covered by a particularly large and thick capstone. There is a small antechamber with a broken capstone.

Presaddfed burial chambers, Bodedern, Anglesey. OS 114: SH 348809. Reached by a minor road off B5109, ½ mile (0.8 km) east of Bodedern. Cadw.

There are two chambers 7 feet (2.1 metres) apart, standing almost on the shore of Llyn Llywennan. One has a capstone on three uprights; the other has uprights only. It is likely that one cairn covered both, as at Dyffryn Ardudwy.

'Roman Steps'. OS 124: SH 657300. Reached by taking the minor road from Llanbedr, 4 miles (6 km) south of Harlech, to the car park at Llyn Cwm Bychan.

Included here because of their popular name, the actual steps may well be medieval, but the trackway, which once ended at Bala, was almost certainly in use during the Roman period and probably well before. It is a very fine walk.

Segontium Roman fort, Caernarfon. OS 115: SH 485624. In Caernarfon. Cadw.

Probably established in AD 78 to guard the Menai Strait, this auxiliary fort was occupied until about AD 395 and underwent considerable modification during that time. Apart from excavated remains, there is a museum on the site set up by the National Museum of Wales, and the site is fully interpreted.

Tre'r Ceiri hillfort, Llanaelhaearn, Lleyn peninsula. OS 123: SH 373446. Path starts on B4417, 1 mile (1.6 km) south-west of Llanaelhaearn.

This is one of the major British hillforts, on the eastern summit of the triple-peaked mountain called Yr Eifl. It was probably founded in the bronze age but there is evidence of occupation through to the Roman period. The extensive enclosure has two entrances in its massive dry-stone boundary wall and contains over one hundred hut foundations, ranging in size from small cells to dwellings 16 feet (4.9 metres) in diameter, indicating a substantial settled community. There are splendid views.

Ty Mawr hut circles, Holyhead. OS 114: SH 212820. On Holyhead Mountain near RSPB car park, South Stack. Cadw.

Reached by an easy path, this extensive series of hut circles probably dates from the Roman occupation, although a much earlier date has been suggested. The stone foundations of about twenty circles survive, some with signs of hearths and slabs for sleeping.

Caernarfon Castle.

4
Castles and monastic buildings

Gwynedd is not abundantly endowed with medieval castles but it does have four of the finest in Britain. In the final years of the thirteenth century Edward I made a determined and successful attempt to subdue the rebellious Welsh, and part of his strategy was to construct a series of imposing castles across North Wales. They were extravagantly expensive and were designed by the outstanding castle architect of the day, Master James of St George. He did not employ a uniform plan: Beaumaris, Caernarfon, Conwy and Harlech have in common enormous defensive strength, but each one is distinctive, and their ruins are substantial enough for the modern visitor to appreciate not only their majestic scale but their aesthetic quality.

The 'Edwardian' castles introduced a more sophisticated design and new defensive techniques. Early castles had been built on the principle of a strongpoint, usually a keep, surrounded by defensive structures like curtain walls, towers and gatehouses. The weakness of this design was the difficulty of defending the walls with a small garrison: a large force would sooner or later breach the walls at some point and attack the keep.

By the time of Edward I castles were being built with the living accommodation *within* the gatehouses and towers, making them as impregnable as possible. In this way the defending force could be concentrated at a few strategic points and be far more effective. The principal apartments were usually in the gatehouse, and the defensive devices were often remarkable. The original design of the King's Gate at Caernarfon was such that attackers would first have to cross a moat, then fight their way through five heavy doors and six portcullises before reaching an inner ditch. While attempting this they would be assailed by arrows and other missiles from skilfully placed apertures and 'murder holes' in the floor above the passageway. There might also be a water gate, which allowed the castle to be supplied by ship in the event of a siege.

Another characteristic of these castles is the distribution of turrets around the curtain wall. Attackers attempting to scale the wall would be caught in a crossfire from the turrets, in which the defenders would be virtually invulnerable, and if the walls were breached each turret became a strongpoint requiring capture. The curtain walls had another useful function: their sheer height and length were impressive and they served as a symbol of power.

The county's other castles are more modest, having been built as native Welsh fortifications in an earlier and simpler style, although most were taken over and developed by Edward I's builders.

Gwynedd has few remaining traces of monastic buildings, although early Celtic Christianity was based strongly on the monastic system (see introduction to chapter 5). The only major ruins of a Celtic monastery are on Ynys Seiriol (Priestholm) off the north-eastern tip of Anglesey, a site which is not normally accessible. The Celtic monasteries were tiny. The prolific growth of English monasteries in the twelfth century was not repeated in Gwynedd, partly because of its remoteness but also because of its political insecurity for Norman monks. Those that were established in the early middle ages never achieved the riches of their English counterparts, and substantial remains are found only at Cymer and Penmon. Nevertheless, the Cistercian abbey of Aberconwy was of great importance and Llewelyn the Great was buried there.

Beaumaris Castle, Beaumaris, Anglesey. Telephone: 0248 810361. Cadw.

Beaumaris was the last of the series built by Edward I – the eighth to be supervised by Master James of St George – and work began in 1295 following the revolt by Madog ap Llewelyn, when Anglesey became a refuge for the rebels. The limestone came from the nearby Penmon quarries, and four hundred masons were employed as well as two thousand other workers. Although its construction occupied about 35 years the castle was never finished and saw no serious action. The mainland of North Wales relied on corn and other food supplies from Anglesey, and one of the castle's functions (together with Caernarfon Castle) was to control the Menai Strait and, if necessary, cut off these essential supplies from any future rebels.

The broad flat site allowed space for concentric walls as well as a wide wet moat. The first line of defence after the moat is an outer wall with twelve towers and two gates, one of

which gave access to a dock so that the castle could be supplied by sea. The inner walls are square in plan and have six towers and two gatehouses, the latter designed as strong points with residential accommodation (the gatehouses were never completed to full height). The curtain walls contain long passages linking the towers.

The remains are substantial and well preserved, and an exhibition explaining Edward I's Welsh castles is housed in the former Chapel Tower.

Caernarfon Castle, Caernarfon. Telephone: 0286 77617. Cadw.

Caernarfon Castle is the greatest of Edward I's castles and has traditional royal links. It was begun in 1283 and took over forty years to build, costing the equivalent of many millions of pounds in modern values. The expense is explained by the fact that it was intended as an official royal residence and seat of government, and Caernarfon became the capital of Wales until 1536. In modern times it has been the scene of the investiture of the last two Princes of Wales.

Because of its special status it was given an unusually ornate quality, with banded masonry and a design based on the walls of Constantinople, which Edward I had seen during a crusade. The site is long and narrow, precluding the use of concentric walls, and the irregularly shaped plan originally consisted of two wards, one incorporating an older castle mound and therefore at a higher level. The high curtain wall has two tiers of passages linking the nine huge polygonal towers and the two massive and powerfully defended gatehouses, which contained the main residential accommodation.

The town walls were built at the same time and substantial lengths remain, including two twin-towered gateways.

Castell y Bere. Signposted off B4405 6½ miles (10 km) north-east of Towyn. Cadw.

The castle is dramatically situated on an isolated rock outcrop overlooking the Dysynni valley and was designed to command several important hill tracks. It was a native Welsh castle, probably started by Prince Llewelyn the Great in 1221 as his headquarters, and was improved by Edward I after its capture by royal forces in 1283. The castle was designed basically as a walled enclosure with a rectangular keep and towers containing apart-

Above: *The courtyard,
Castell y Bere.*

Left: *Conwy Castle,
showing Telford's road
bridge in the fore-
ground and Robert
Stephenson's railway
bridge on the left.*

ments. Surviving carving shows that it was probably richly ornamented, as befitted the residence of a prince. Although little is left standing, the foundations and earthworks, as well as the location, make this a rewarding site to visit.

Conwy Castle, Conwy. Telephone: 0492 592358. Cadw.

Conwy is reckoned to be one of the finest castles in Europe. It was begun in 1283 by Edward I after he had gained control of the Conwy valley from Llewelyn ap Gruffudd and was largely complete by 1287. To provide space, the abbey of Aberconwy was removed and resited further up the valley.

Like Caernarfon, Conwy Castle stands on an elongated site that allowed only one set of curtain walls. It had water on three sides, and the near-rectangular plan provided for two wards separated by a powerful cross-wall. The outer ward contained the long Great Hall, while the smaller inner ward, with its own drawbridge and gatehouse, was reserved for the private royal quarters – luxurious by the standards of the time. The outstanding feature of the castle is the series of eight huge towers

in the curtain walls, each providing living accommodation on several floors. The town walls were an integral part of the defensive scheme and almost the entire length remains, fortified by 21 towers and three twin-towered gateways.

There is a visitor centre at the entrance.

Criccieth Castle, Criccieth. Telephone: 0766 522227. Cadw.

Like Castell y Bere, this was a castle created by Llewelyn ap Iorwerth, 'the Great', and later taken over and improved by the English. It stands on a rocky seaside peninsula in Criccieth. The inner ward, including the twin-towered gatehouse, was probably built by Llewelyn ap Iorwerth. The castle was modified by his grandson, Llewelyn ap Gruffudd, and further altered by Edward I and Edward II.

Cymer Abbey. Signposted off A494, 2 miles (3 km) north-west of Dolgellau. Cadw.

Like all Cistercian abbeys this was built in a remote spot, but it is now on the fringe of a caravan site. It was founded in 1198-9, and the main ruins are those of an arcade of the small thirteenth-century abbey church.

The beach and castle at Criccieth.

Cymer Abbey.

Dolbadarn Castle. At the head of Llyn Padarn, ¹/₂ mile (0.8 km) south-east of Llanberis. Cadw.

Dolbadarn was another of Llewelyn the Great's castles, built in the early thirteenth century to command the entrance to the Llanberis pass. It was abandoned after the defeat of the Welsh by Edward I. The main feature of the surviving ruins is the cylindrical Great Tower, almost 50 feet (15 metres) high, of three storeys and entered at first-floor level. A square projection at the rear housed a latrine.

Dolwyddelan Castle. 1 mile (1.6 km) west of Dolwyddelan on A470 between Betws-y-coed and Blaenau Ffestiniog. Cadw.

Like Dolbadarn Castle, this fortification was designed to command a strategic route into the heartland of the Welsh princes. The castle stands on a natural ridge offering effective protection, although ditches were cut into the rock for extra defence. Llewelyn ap Iorwerth (Prince Llewelyn the Great) is reputed to have been born here in 1173, and it became an important headquarters of the princes in the thirteenth century. Its building history is not entirely clear, but it seems that the two-storey rectangular keep of the late twelfth century had an extra floor added in the fifteenth century. This still stands, but little remains of the curtain wall that surrounded it. The western tower is later. Despite the scanty ruins, it is a fine site to visit.

Harlech Castle, Harlech. Telephone: 0766 780552. Cadw.

Edward I's castle at Harlech was begun in 1283 and completed seven years later. It was designed to take advantage of a steep-sided promontory rock (above the sea when it was built) with a dry moat protecting the landward side. It is concentric in plan with a low outer wall encircling immensely powerful inner defences. These consist of a high curtain wall with massive towers at the four corners and a huge gatehouse containing the main residential apartments. There is evidence here of three sets of doors and three portcullises. There was further accommodation in the other towers, and foundations show the position of the Great Hall and kitchens. As at the other Gwynedd castles of this period, the castle could be supplied by ship.

Dolwyddelan Castle.

*The great gateway of
Harlech Castle.*

The castle saw action during the Owain Glyndwr revolt, when the garrison was starved into submission, allowing Glyndwr to occupy the castle for four years. Later it was garrisoned for the Lancastrians during the Wars of the Roses, and its commander, Dafydd ap Ifan, had the distinction of being the last to surrender to the Yorkists. His eight-year stand inspired the song 'Men of Harlech'.

Penmon Priory, Anglesey. 3¹/₂ miles (6 km) north-east of Beaumaris.

The site of the priory is traditionally associated with St Seiriol, a sixth-century Celtic saint, although the present building (in use as a parish church) dates from no earlier than the twelfth and thirteenth centuries. The church is primitive and mysterious, with some interesting carving over the south doorway and on two of the tower arches. (The designs on the doorway show a combination of Celtic interlaced patterns and the more angular Norman decoration.) A cross preserved inside is believed to be of the early eleventh century, as is the font. Attached to the church, and occupied, is the former prior's house, and the remains of the refectory stand nearby. A path leads to the secluded St Seiriol's Well with a stone structure, restored in the eighteenth century, that is popularly supposed to have been his cell. Also nearby is the shell of a remarkable sixteenth-century dovecot, not connected with the priory.

Capel Peniel, the striking chapel built in 1810 at Tremadog.

5
Churches and chapels

Any visitor familiar with English churches is bound to become aware of the very different Christian tradition that produced the parish churches of Gwynedd. The most obvious difference is the variety of dedications to saints unknown outside Wales – St Pabo, St Iestyn, St Illtud and so on.

Christianity was introduced to Britain in the later years of the Roman empire and took hold among the Celtic peoples. During the post-Roman period, when most of England was occupied by pagan invaders who virtually extinguished the faith, the isolated Celtic Christianity in the extreme north and west of Britain and in Ireland continued to spread. It is believed that the early Welsh church was strongly influenced by refugees from Gaul, who brought with them the idea that Christian faith was best expressed by the life of the hermit. At the same time there was an influx of wandering missionaries from Ireland.

The result was the emergence of the Celtic saints. These men walked from place to place, preaching and leading very ascetic lives. Whenever they encountered a particularly fruitful area they would construct a *llan* – not normally a church building but an enclosure in which they lived their solitary lives and which came to be regarded as holy ground. Often the site would be developed by followers of the saint as a small monastery, and this would usually lead to the building of a *clas* or mother church, with pastoral responsibilities for a wide area.

The *llan* in which the church was built would be identified by the name of the saint who had established it, and this led to the enormous number of Welsh place-names with the *Llan* prefix followed by a name. By studying the distribution of place-names it is possible to build up a picture of the itineraries and areas of influence of the principal saints.

26

The original Romano-British custom of government by bishops was not forgotten in Wales, and the Bangor diocese was founded in the sixth century by St Deiniol, the first bishop of Gwynedd. When missionaries arrived from Rome in the seventh century with the aim of converting the Anglo-Saxons, the Celtic church was strongly organised, and Roman ideas had little influence until after the Norman invasion, when the Welsh were forced into greater uniformity. The saints were not forgotten, however, and their dedications survived.

The Welsh language involves mutations that can produce a slight difference between the name of a place and the name of its saint. Thus St Pabo's church is at Llanbabo. Similar examples are St Cybi/Llangybi, St Cadwaladr/Llangadwaladr and St Twrog/Llandwrog. Mutations can also disguise more familiar names: for example, Llansantffraid is a dedication to the Irish saint Braid or Bridget, and Llanbedr is a dedication to St Peter. The many place-names beginning 'Llanfair' derive from 'Mair', the Virgin Mary.

One would not expect to find very early churches in Gwynedd, partly because the prolific wave of Norman church-building failed to touch this part of Wales but also because the primitive Celtic churches that did survive were replaced during the middle ages. Nevertheless many of these medieval churches copied the basic design of their Celtic predecessors – a rectangular plan with no structural division between nave and chancel, and with a bellcote rather than a tower. A large number of these tiny 'single-cell' churches survive in Gwynedd. In places which prospered during the nineteenth century (for example, as centres of industry or tourism) the medieval churches were replaced in turn by new and larger buildings by Victorian architects, and the majority of Gwynedd's churches were the subject of nineteenth-century restoration.

Regrettably it is common nowadays to find churches locked, though there is often a notice indicating the keyholder, especially if the building is of historical importance. The question of whether a remote church will be open can sometimes be answered by inquiring at the vicarage or rectory in the nearest large village. There has never been a tradition of leaving nonconformist chapels open to the public, which is why they do not figure largely in this gazetteer. Some chapels of architectural or historical importance are, however, included. Anyone seeking insight into nineteenth-

century Welsh religious history, particularly the nonconformist tradition, is recommended to visit Yr Hen Gapel at Tre'r Ddol in Dyfed, 10 miles (16 km) south-west of Machynlleth on A487 (telephone: 0970 86407). It is a private collection housed in an old chapel which was the starting point of one of the famous nineteenth-century religious revivals.

Aberdaron: St Hywin. Beside the beach in the village.

Aberdaron was the embarkation point for pilgrims making their way to Bardsey Island, a place regarded as particularly holy, and they probably used St Hywin's church as a shelter while awaiting a boat across the dangerous channel. The Norman features are the west doorway and north nave wall; an extension in the fourteenth century added a south aisle. A new church for Aberdaron, begun in the 1840s, aroused such an outcry that it was abandoned in favour of restoring St Hywin's.

Aberffraw (Anglesey): St Mary Tal-y-llyn. OS 114: SH 367728. 2¹/₂ miles (4 km) along a minor road to Gwalchmai.

This tiny isolated roadside church or chapel has architectural features of the twelfth, sixteenth and seventeenth centuries, together with eighteenth-century pews and other fittings. A restoration in the 1960s preserved its unadorned medieval character.

Abersoch: Capel Newydd. OS 123: SH 286309. Off B4413, 2¹/₂ miles (4 km) north-west of Abersoch. (Key probably at the house at the lane junction.)

This is believed to be the oldest nonconformist chapel in North Wales, built in 1769, abandoned in 1872, but restored in the 1950s complete with its authentic interior.

Bangor: The Cathedral.

The diocese of Bangor, established in the sixth century, is the oldest in England and Wales. The Cathedral developed from a monastic foundation, but the original buildings were destroyed in Owain Glyndwr's rebellion, and the earliest surviving parts of the present structure date from the rebuilding during the fifteenth and sixteenth centuries. It was the subject of extensive restoration between 1868 and 1880 by Sir Gilbert Scott and his son, and this has given it a largely Victorian character. There are some interesting tombs and memorials, but the outstanding feature is a fine fifteenth-century wooden representation of Christ.

Bethesda

The village is named after the impressive white-fronted chapel in the main street (founded in 1820 and rebuilt in 1840), and the other examples in the village, particularly the Siloam Chapel of 1872, are imposing enough to indicate the strength of the nonconformist tradition in the industrial villages during the second half of the nineteenth century. The parish church is insignificant by contrast.

Brithdir: St Mark. OS 124: SH 764184. Off A470, 3 miles (5 km) east of Dolgellau.

This most intriguing church was built in the 1890s at the expense of a local benefactress and designed by the architect Henry Wilson, who was scrupulous in using local materials for the exterior. The roof, sweeping down from the ridge almost to head height, is the outstanding architectural feature, and colour is used effectively inside the church, where the

pulpit, reredos and altar display the copper work that was one of Wilson's specialities. The chancel stalls are carved with animals.

Clynnog Fawr: St Beuno. OS 123: SH 414497. On A499, 10 miles (16 km) south of Caernarfon.

This was a Celtic *clas* church that became a collegiate foundation in the middle ages. Its importance was due to the fact that it housed the shrine of St Beuno, one of the most important Celtic saints, and wealth accumulated from pilgrims helped to build the present impressive building in the fifteenth century. The site of the saint's shrine is marked by a sixteenth-century chapel connected to the tower (a feature known as a *capel y bedd* and seen also at Llaneilian and Holyhead). The church itself is a fine Perpendicular structure, with generous windows, battlements and pinnacles, and the chancel has interesting stalls with misericords. On display is the formidable chest in which pilgrims' offerings were secured.

The church of St Beuno, Clynnog Fawr.

Conwy: St Mary (parish church).

When Edward I built Conwy Castle he cleared a site by moving the Cistercian abbey up the valley. The abbey church, however, remained to serve the parish. Apart from the three lancet windows in the tower and a good late Norman doorway, little of the original structure remains. The outstanding feature here is the superb late fifteenth-century rood screen, and, as in most town churches, there are some notable memorials. There is a long-standing tradition that a tomb on the south side of the church inspired Wordsworth's famous poem 'We are Seven'.

Dolgellau: St Mary (parish church).

Eighteenth-century churches are rare in Gwynedd, but St Mary's dates from 1716 and has survived virtually in its original form. It is in local stone, and the interior has a nave roof supported on wooden columns. The large windows would originally have contained clear glass, and the present stained glass (some very striking) is Victorian. A reminder of the original church is a fourteenth-century effigy of a member of a local family.

Dolwyddelan: The Old Church. In the village on A470 between Betws-y-coed and Blaenau Ffestiniog.

St Gwyddelan's has a sixteenth-century nave and chancel with a later south chapel. The principal features are the original rood screen and a memorial brass (1525) to the builder of the church, but the main pleasure here is the authentic primitive quality of the building.

Holyhead: St Cybi.

The large cruciform church stands within the town, bounded by walls of a Roman fort. Its size reflects its history as a Celtic *clas* church and later a collegiate establishment. It was rebuilt in the late fifteenth century in battlemented and pinnacled style, and elaborate carvings of the period decorate the south transept parapet. The Victorian south chapel contains stained glass by Burne-Jones and William Morris.

Llanallgo (Anglesey): Capel Lligwy. OS 114: SH 499864. ¹/₂ mile (0.8 km) north of Llanallgo. Cadw.

The roofless shell of the very simple church probably dates from the first half of the twelfth century, although the south chapel is much later.

Llanbabo (Anglesey): St Pabo. OS 114: SH 378868.

The church stands next to the Llyn Alaw reservoir and is noted for a fourteenth-century carving of St Pabo, similar to that of Llaniestyn (below) and probably by the same artist.

Llanbedr: Salem Chapel. OS 124: SH 603274. Beside minor road leading off A496 at Llanbedr, south of Harlech.

This cottage-like Baptist chapel with an eighteenth-century interior was immortalised in a popular painting by the Edwardian artist Curnow Vosper.

Llandwrog: St Twrog. OS 123: SH 452561. Off A499, 6 miles (10 km) south of Caernarfon.

The church of 1860 is noteworthy for its good nineteenth-century fittings and its unusual arrangement of pews as in a college chapel. It was the estate church of Glynllifon Park, and there are some interesting monuments.

Llanegryn: Saints Mary and Egryn. OS 124: SH 596057.

On a commanding site overlooking the Dysynni valley, the church is predominantly a Victorian restoration, but it has retained one of the most beautiful rood screens in North Wales.

Llaneilian (Anglesey): St Eilian. OS 114: SH 469929. 2 miles (3 km) east of Amlwch.

Externally the church is typically Perpendicular in style, with a low-pitched roof and battlements, although the squat tower dates from the twelfth century and fits rather awkwardly with the rest of the building. The main interest here is in the fittings, which include a fine fifteenth-century rood screen and loft and chancel stalls of the same period. An unusual oblique passage leads to St Eilian's Chapel, or *capel y bedd*, supposedly the site of the saint's well. Among several interesting objects displayed is the strong-box used for pilgrims' offerings.

Llanengan: St Einion. OS 123: SH 294270. 1¹/₂ miles (2 km) south-west of Abersoch.

Llanengan has a particularly splendid church – not suprisingly, because it housed the shrine of St Einion. The building was reconstructed and enlarged with a tower in the early sixteenth century, and its most notable features are the two rood screens (one complete with loft) in the nave and south aisle and the octagonal font.

Llangadwaladr (Anglesey): St Cadwaladr. OS 114: SH 383693. Beside A4080, 1¹/₂ miles (2 km) east of Aberffraw.

The church contains the grave slab of King Cadfan (died AD *c.625) and a remarkable fifteenth-century east window representing the Crucifixion and St Cadwaladr. The south chapel (mid seventeenth-century) and north chapel (Victorian) both have notable monuments of their periods.

Llangelynnin Old Church: St Celynin. OS 115: SH 752737. Off B5106, 4 miles (6 km) south-west of Conwy.

This lonely unspoilt church is reached by the track to Garnedd-wen Farm, where the key is kept. The fifteenth-century chancel has a barrel roof and is divided from the Elizabethan north chapel by a screen. Texts in Welsh adorn the walls. (The new Llangelynnin church of 1840, at SH 772735, is also worth visiting.)

Llangwnnadl: St Gwynhoydl. OS 123: SH 208333. Off B4417, 10 miles (16 km) south-west of Nefyn.

Attractively situated well away from the village, the church is surprisingly spacious, its medieval nave having been enlarged to north and south in the early sixteenth century. A sixth-century incised stone is set in the south wall, and there is an octagonal sixteenth-century font.

Llangybi: St Cybi's Well. OS 123: SH 427413. 5 miles (8 km) north-east of Pwllheli. Cadw.

This is not a church but a notable religious site. St Cybi traditionally arrived from Cornwall in the sixth century AD and established a monastery at Caer Gybi fort. His well attracted pilgrims throughout the middle ages and later in the eighteenth century, when it was exploited as a spa. The site now has an eighteenth-century cottage, two well-chambers and a detached latrine building.

Llaniestyn (Anglesey): St Iestyn. OS 114: SH 585796. ¹/₂ mile (0.8 km) east of Llanddona.

The church is small and L-shaped, with a carved Norman south doorway and a remarkable relief carving of the saint, created in the fourteenth century.

Llanllyfni: Capel Ebenezer. 7 miles (11 km) south of Caernarfon on A487.

Like many nonconformist chapels this dates from the early nineteenth century, but it is uncommon in having retained box-pews and other features of its original interior.

Llanrhwydrys. OS 114: SH 322932.

Now totally isolated near the cliffs west of Cemlyn Bay, this church makes a good objective for a coastal walk (car park at SH 328934). It has a twelfth-century nave with a gallery of the 1770s and a thirteenth-century chancel.

Llanrhychwyn: St Rhychwyn. OS 115: SH 775616. 2 miles (3 km) due west of Llanrwst.

Reached by a forest lane, the church has a primitive atmosphere enhanced by whitewash, slate floors and unadorned oak roofs. The Norman south doorway leads into the twelfth-century nave; the chancel was added in the fifteenth century and the north aisle in the sixteenth.

Llanrwst: Gwydir Uchaf Chapel. Signposted off B5106, 1 mile (1.6 km) south-west of Llanrwst. Admission charge. Cadw.

The chapel was built in 1673 for the use of the Wynn family at the nearby Gwydir Castle. It is a tiny Gothic structure of considerable charm, and the interior features some interesting carving and a painted ceiling noted for its ambitious but naive workmanship.

Llanrwst: St Grwst.

A much restored fifteenth-century building, the church deserves a visit for its superb rood screen and loft and also for the Gwydir Chapel (not to be confused with the nearby Gwydir Uchaf Chapel). This seventeenth-century structure is the memorial chapel of the local Wynn family and contains some fine and interesting monuments.

Penmon (Anglesey).

The Priory Church is described in chapter 4.

Pistyll: St Beuno. OS 123: SH 328423. Off B4417, 2 miles (3 km) north-east of Nefyn.

This was another pilgrims' church, a tiny austere building with a fine timber roof and traces of a wall-painting.

Tremadog: Capel Peniel.

Included as part of William Madocks's planned town (see chapter 12), this chapel of 1810, with its impressive portico, is a good example of the adaptation of formal classical features to chapel architecture.

Penrhyn Castle and park.

6
Houses and gardens

Aberconwy House, Conwy LL32 8AY. Telephone: 0492 592246. National Trust.
This is a rare survival in Gwynedd of a late medieval merchant's house. Its two lower floors are of stone but the top floor is timber-framed and jettied. It houses an exhibition on the theme of Conwy's past and also a National Trust shop.

Bodnant Garden, Tal-y-Cafn, Colwyn Bay, Clwyd LL28 5RE. Telephone: 0492 650460. National Trust.
The garden at Bodnant, first laid out in 1875, is world-famous both for its colourful displays throughout the year and for the magnificent views from its 80 acre (32 ha) site above the Conwy river. It has two contrasting areas: formal terrace gardens close to the house and an informally landscaped 'wild garden' in the small river valley below. A famous feature is the artificial canal closed off by the charming Pin Mill. Specialities here are magnolias, rhododendrons, camellias and azaleas. Facilities include a refreshment pavilion and an extensive nursery with plants for sale.

Bryn Bras Castle, Llanrug, Llanberis, near Caernarfon LL55 4RE. Telephone: 0286 870210.
Like nearby Penrhyn Castle but on a smaller scale, this is an example of a nineteenth-century mock castle, but built for a wealthy solicitor. The architect may have been Thomas Hopper, the designer of Penrhyn. The house started as a modest farmhouse and was enlarged and transformed in fanciful Gothic style in the 1830s. In addition to the interesting interior the 30 acres (12 ha) of grounds are open, providing a blend of formality and extensive woodland, leading to a mountain walk with views.

Cochwillan Old Hall, Talybont, Bangor. Telephone: 0248 364608.
The house is privately owned and open only by appointment, but it is included here because any visitor interested in architecture is likely to want to see this rare Gwynedd example of a hall-house of the mid fifteenth century. It was used as a barn for many years, but the Great Hall has now been splendidly restored. Its outstanding feature is its carved hammerbeam roof.

CHAPTER 6

Gwydir Castle, Llanrwst. Telephone: 0492 640261.

The original fortified mansion dated from the sixteenth century and was enlarged and modernised steadily during the next two hundred years as the home of the Wynn family, who were highly influential locally and nationally. Following a major fire in the 1920s it had to be heavily restored, but some original interior features remain.

Parc Glynllifon, Llandwrog, Caernarfon LL54 5DY. Telephone: 0286 830222. Gwynedd County Council.

The gardens and woodlands of the former home of Lord Newborough have been restored and now contain several additional attractions, such as landscape sculpture, the eighteenth-century private barracks known as Fort Williamsburg and restored estate workshops, and there is an information centre. The house, built in 1836 and used in recent years as a college, is not open.

Penarth Fawr Medieval House, Pwllheli. OS 123: SH 419376. Off A497, 3 miles (5 km) east of Pwllheli. Cadw.

This is a rare opportunity to see the structure of a fifteenth-century hall-house, complete with roof timbers and a spere-truss, the timber screen which divided the hall from the service quarters. A seventeenth-century modernisation produced the fireplaces and large windows. (See also Cochwillan Old Hall.)

Penrhyn Castle, Bangor LL57 4HN. Telephone: 0248 353084. National Trust.

This extraordinary mansion was built by Thomas Hopper for George Pennant, later Lord Penrhyn, who owned the highly profitable quarries at Bethesda. A medieval fortified house originally stood on the site. This was incorporated into an eighteenth-century mock castle, the 'great hall' of which was the basis for the present house, built between 1827 and 1840. The style is vaguely neo-Norman, and the vast irregular plan includes an array of

Penarth Fawr near Pwllheli, a hall-house of the early fifteenth century.

impressive castellated towers, round and rectangular, culminating in a huge keep. The Norman theme is continued in much of the interior carving, particularly on the Grand Staircase, and the rooms are vast and extravagantly rich. There are extensive grounds with fine trees and terraced gardens. Additional attractions include a collection of Old Masters in the dining room, an industrial railway museum and a doll museum.

Plas Glyn-y-Weddw, Llanbedrog, Pwllheli LL53 7TT. Telephone: 0758 740763.

The house is a mansion of 1856 in the Gothic style with a notable Victorian interior. The glass-domed entrance hall is particularly fine, with a hammerbeam roof, a magnificent staircase and galleries and a large stained glass window. It became an art gallery as long ago as 1896 but fell into disuse until its restoration by the present owners in 1979. It now houses a gallery of paintings for viewing or purchase, and there is a programme of special demonstrations and events. The additional facilities include a Victorian tearoom and shop.

Plas Mawr, High Street, Conwy. Telephone: 0492 593413. Royal Cambrian Academy of Art.

This is a fine example of a well preserved late sixteenth-century house, built by Robert Wynn of Gwydir, near Llanrwst. It is stone-built with stepped gables and has the fashionable Elizabethan H plan, although the pediments over the mullioned windows show a classical influence. There is a courtyard to the rear and another to the side, separating the mansion from its gatehouse. The interior is notable for its fireplaces and wealth of plasterwork. It is leased by the Royal Cambrian Academy of Art, who use it as their headquarters and gallery.

Plas Newydd, Llanfairpwll, Anglesey LL61 6EQ. Telephone: 0248 714795. National Trust.

Standing in grounds running down to the Menai Strait, Plas Newydd, the home of the Marquesses of Anglesey, is an elegant house of 1795-1806 by James Wyatt and Joseph Potter, who produced a fusion of classical and Gothic styles. The dining room is famous for a vast mural by Rex Whistler, whose work is remembered in a special exhibition. The first Marquess distinguished himself at the battle of Waterloo, and a small military museum has relics of the occasion. The grounds contain fine shrubs and trees, and in spring the rhododendrons, azaleas and camellias have a special appeal. The facilities include a tearoom and a shop.

Plas yn Rhiw, Rhiw, Pwllheli LL53 8AB. Telephone: 075888 219. National Trust.

This is a medieval house, extended in the seventeenth, eighteenth and nineteenth centuries. The interior contains some good furniture and domestic bygones, but the outstanding attraction is the garden, laid out informally in traditional country style and commanding stunning views over Cardigan Bay.

Ty Mawr Wybrnant, Penmachno, Betws-y-coed LL25 0HJ. Telephone: 06903 213. Signposted from Penmachno, 4 miles (6 km) south of Betws-y-coed on the B4406. National Trust.

Ty Mawr has been restored to its seventeenth-century condition. The cottage was the birthplace, in 1545, of Bishop William Morgan, who first translated the whole Bible into Welsh; his translation appeared in 1588 and is considered to have been the most important single achievement in establishing the modern Welsh language. Morgan went on to become Bishop of St Asaph.

Exhibits on display in the audio-visual entertainments room, Museum of Childhood, Beaumaris.

7
Museums

BANGOR
Museum of Welsh Antiquities and Art Gallery, The Old Canonry, Fford Gwynedd, Bangor.

The museum covers a wide range of local history from prehistoric material to domestic bygones and paintings. The Art Gallery, in the same building, houses touring exhibitions and shows by local artists.

BEAUMARIS
Beaumaris Courthouse and Gaol, Beaumaris. Inquiries to Gwynedd Archives and Museum Service at Llangefni, telephone 0248 750262 extension 269, or at Caernarfon, telephone 0286 4121.

The gaol was constructed in 1829 as the county prison with up-to-date fittings in the spirit of Peel's Prison Reform Act. Demoted to becoming a police station and local lock-up in 1878, it escaped modernisation, and the visitor can see many of its original features, including the punishment and condemned cells, a treadwheel used for pumping water and the door from which condemned prisoners took

their final walk. Also on view is a private collection of police memorabilia.

The courthouse stands opposite the castle and can be visited when not in use. It is an authentic Victorian structure with most of its original fittings.

Museum of Childhood, 1 Castle Street, Beaumaris LL58 8AP. Telephone: 0248 712498.

The museum is Robert Brown's private collection of over two thousand items, occupying nine rooms and including rare toys and other bygones illustrating childhood and family life. This museum was moved to Beaumaris from Menai Bridge in 1985.

BEDDGELERT
Sygun Copper Mine, Beddgelert LL55 4NE. Telephone: 0766 86595. 1 mile (1.6 km) from the village off A498 (Capel Curig) road.

This site, which closed in 1903, is the only one of Gwynedd's copper mines to have been reopened. It now provides underground tours through the remarkable caverns left by the old

34

workings, with multilingual audio presentations explaining the production methods.
Working conditions have been imaginatively
reconstructed. A visitor centre displays photographs and mining artefacts, and there is a
souvenir shop and cafe.

BETWS-Y-COED
Conwy Valley Railway Museum, The Old
Goods Yard, Betws-y-coed LL24 0AL.
Telephone: 06902 568.

The museum has exhibits on railways generally but especially on those of North Wales,
together with a model railway. Steam trains
operate a scenic ride daily throughout the
season.

Motor Museum, Betws Farm, Betws-y-coed
LL24 0AH. Telephone: 06902 632.

This is a private collection of vintage and
exotic cars, with a souvenir and model shop
and refreshment facilities.

BLAENAU FFESTINIOG
Gloddfa Ganol Slate Mine, Blaenau
Ffestiniog LL41 3NB. Telephone: 0766
830664.

Reputed to be the world's largest slate mine,
Gloddfa Ganol has been reopened to provide
underground tours with reconstructions of
mining in progress. Land-Rover tours of the
extensive site are also available. Other attrac-

Viewing Llechwedd Slate Caverns by tram.

*Westland Whirlwind rescue helicopter at Air
World, Caernarfon*

tions include a working slate mill, restored
miners' cottages, the quarry railway, an exhibition hall and refreshment facilities.

Llechwedd Slate Caverns, Blaenau Ffestiniog
LL41 3NB. Telephone: 0766 830306.

Two underground tours are provided: by
tram into the side of the mountain to see
tableaux of all the processes of slate production, and by special vehicle into one of the
deeper levels, where the social life of the
miners is recreated by a sound and light presentation. Surface attractions include Victorian shops, a 'Slates to the Sea' museum,
railway exhibits, an exhibition on David
Francis, the 'Blind Harpist', in the cottage
where he lived, and craft demonstrations. There
is a range of refreshment facilities.

CAERNARFON
Air World, Caernarfon Airport, Dinas Dinlle,
Caernarfon LL54 5TP. Telephone: 0286
830800.

A large indoor museum contains 'hands on'
aeroplanes, helicopters, engines and a pro-
cedural trainer. There are over two hundred
model aircraft and exhibitions of aviation his-

tory and wartime nostalgia. A cinema shows films on the theme of aviation and there is the Airworld adventure playground for children. Pleasure flights are available in a Cessna or a vintage de Havilland Rapide.

Seiont II Maritime Museum, Victoria Dock, Caernarfon. Telephone: 0248 712528.

Seiont II is the restored coal-fired steam dredger that forms the centrepiece of the museum, which also includes the last of the Menai Strait ferries and exhibits in a quayside museum building, all designed to present a picture of the maritime life and history of the area. The museum is run by the Seiont II Maritime Trust, a registered charity, membership of which is open to all.

CLYNNOG FAWR
Museum of Welsh Country Life, Felin Faesog, Tai'n Lon, Clynnog Fawr. Telephone: 0286 86311. Signposted off A487 and A499, 10 miles (16 km) south of Caernarfon.

Housed in a restored watermill, the museum contains agricultural and craft bygones, illustrating, among other things, the clogmaker's trade and the life of women and children. Antiques and books are on sale and there is a cafe.

CONWY
Aberconwy House. See chapter 6.

Plas Mawr. See chapter 6.

CORRIS
Corris Railway Museum, Station Yard, Corris, Machynlleth. SY20 9SH. Telephone: 065473 343.

This small museum is operated by the Corris Railway Society, which is dedicated to reviving the narrow-gauge line that once carried slate down to the Dyfi estuary.

HARLECH
Chwarel Hen Slate Caverns, Llanfair, Harlech. Telephone: 0766 780247.

The reopened slate mine provides guided tours through illuminated underground workings with an explanation of extraction methods. There is a cafe and craft shop.

HOLYHEAD
Holyhead Maritime Museum, Rhos-y-Gaer Avenue, Holyhead LL65 2BE. Telephone: 0407 762816.

The museum covers the seafaring history of western Anglesey and particularly the port of Holyhead, with special emphasis on the life-

The Seiont II Maritime Museum, Caernarfon.

The pumped storage power station at Dinorwig.

boat and coastguard service, shipwrecks, lighthouses and the whaling industry. Photographs, plans, ship models, figureheads and marine tools are displayed.

LLANBERIS
The Power of Wales, Llanberis, Caernarfon LL55 4UR. Telephone: 0286 870636.
Operated jointly by the National Museum of Wales and the National Grid Company, this is a series of sophisticated audio-visual presentations illustrating the more vivid episodes of

The Welsh Slate Museum, Llanberis.

Welsh history from prehistoric times, and also focusing on the generation of electrical power at the nearby Dinorwig pumped storage scheme. Other facilities include an exhibition gallery, a Natural Science Theatre and a shop.

Welsh Slate Museum, Y Gilfach Ddu, Llanberis, Caernarfon LL55 4TY. Telephone: 0286 870630.
Housed in the former Dinorwic quarry workshops, which are a fine example of dignified functional architecture, the museum has

37

displays of original equipment and presentations explaining the quarrying process. There are also demonstrations of techniques such as slate splitting.

LLANDUDNO

Oriel Mostyn (Mostyn Art Gallery), 12 Vaughan Street, Llandudno. Telephone: 0492 79201.

The gallery houses monthly exhibitions by artists with Welsh connections or producing work with relevance to Wales.

LLANYSTUMDWY

Lloyd George Museum and Highgate Cottage, Llanystumdwy, Criccieth. Telephone: 0766 522071 or 0286 4121 extension 2098.

The museum displays memorabilia of David Lloyd George (1863-1945), the former Liberal Prime Minister, who had close connections with the village. The building was designed by his friend, the architect Sir Clough Williams-Ellis, to house objects given to Lloyd George by foreign leaders but has been greatly extended

and a lecture theatre has been added.

Highgate Cottage, close by, where Lloyd George lived as a boy with his uncle, is open to the public. It has been restored and refurnished as it would have been in the 1860s.

NEFYN

Lleyn Historical and Maritime Museum, Old St Mary's Church, Church Street, Nefyn LL53 6LE. Telephone: 0758 720206.

The museum has displays illustrating the seafaring and industrial life of the local community from the early nineteenth century to the present day.

PORTHMADOG

Porthmadog Maritime Museum, Oakley Number 1 Wharf, The Harbour, Porthmadog. Telephone: 0766 512864 or 513736.

The last remaining slate shed on the quay houses displays showing the activities of Gwynedd's seafarers and the achievements of Porthmadog's shipbuilders. The rescue services are strongly featured and a former Barmouth lifeboat is one of the exhibits.

The Lloyd George Museum and statue of Lloyd George at Llanystumdwy.

The view of Telford's Menai suspension bridge from the island church of Llandysilio.

8
Industrial archaeology

Former industrial sites now open to the public as museums or interpretative centres are listed in chapter 7. The standard-gauge and narrow-gauge railways are described in chapter 9, but some notable railway features are included below.

HARBOUR WORKS
Holyhead

There is an early nineteenth-century custom house and harbour office. The Admiralty Pier (1821) is by John Rennie. The breakwater, with the lighthouse at its end, was completed in 1873.

ROADS

The outstanding survivals are the work of Thomas Telford, who, in the early years of the nineteenth century, was commissioned to supervise the construction of the London-Holyhead road and also to improve the Chester-Holyhead road along the north coast. The major new work on the London-Holyhead road (now the A5) was the section west of Shrewsbury, which had never been modernised for stage-coaches, and Telford undertook to construct a route on which no gradient would be greater than 1 in 20. His achieve-ment is exemplified in the gentle rise from Betws-y-coed to Capel Curig and the finely engineered road through the Nant Ffrancon pass between Capel Curig and Bethesda, where he replaced a route established earlier by Lord Penrhyn. The road also involved pioneering work in bridge-building. Some of the main features of the London-Holyhead and Chester-Holyhead roads are described below.

Betws-y-coed: Waterloo Bridge

Telford was a master of cast iron, and his elegant bridge over the Conwy is still in use. The spandrels are decorated with leeks, roses, thistles and shamrocks, and the span bears the proud inscription: 'This arch was constructed in the same year the Battle of Waterloo was fought.'

Conwy: suspension bridge

This was opened in 1826. The crossing of the Conwy estuary was the major obstacle on the Chester-Holyhead road (previously it had been necessary to cross by ferry) and Telford chose to use the same type of bridge that he was simultaneously constructing across the Menai Strait. The only feasible crossing point was next to the castle, so he added some

39

uncharacteristic decoration in the form of castellated towers at each end of the 327 foot (100 metre) span. The bridge is rightly admired, but the task of building the 2000 foot (610 metre) approach embankment is often overlooked. At the time of writing the bridge was closed for renovation, but it is normally open to pedestrians.

Holyhead: Stanley Embankment
Faced with the problem of the silted channel between Anglesey and Holy Island, Telford refused to divert his road south to the Four Mile Bridge, the existing crossing at the narrowest point. Instead he designed the massive Stanley Embankment, 1300 yards (1188 metres) long and 16 feet (4.8 metres) high, on a base that tapered from 114 feet (34.7 metres) at the bottom to 34 feet (10.4 metres) at the top. Remarkably the formidable project took only a year to build.

Llanfairpwll: tollhouse
Telford was in the habit of designing the smallest details of his roads, including the milestones, the tollgates and the tollhouses. All the Holyhead Road tollhouses were built to a similar pattern and one is preserved here complete with its list of tolls.

Lord Penrhyn's road
This interesting road, pre-dating Telford and designed to carry slates from the Bethesda quarries, can be followed from a stile by the climbing shop in Capel Curig to the camp site at OS 114: SH 685600, and picked up again at the western end of Llyn Ogwen, where it descends on the opposite side of the valley as a minor road joining the A5 near the quarries.

Menai Bridge
This pioneering venture, completed in 1825, is regarded as one of Telford's supreme achievements. Hitherto travellers between Anglesey and the mainland had been forced to rely on ferries which were dangerous in the treacherous currents and subject to long periods of cancellation during bad weather. There had been previous designs for bridges, but they had foundered on the Admiralty requirement that the height should be above that of the tallest navy ship and that there should be no obstacles in the strait, even during building. Given these restrictions, a suspension bridge was the only possibility, but the technology had been tried only on small-

Thomas Telford, 1757-1834.

scale structures. Telford's plan for a bridge 579 feet (176 metres) long would make it the largest suspension bridge in the world, and the 100 feet (30.5 metres) of clearance would require towers 153 feet (46.6 metres) high.

Work on building the towers started in 1819, and anchorage points for the suspension chains were created by tunnelling into solid rock at each end and installing massive iron frames. Telford specified sixteen chains to support the road platform, and on a day in April 1825 he supervised the task of hoisting the first of them on to the towers from a huge raft anchored below. The task required capstans each manned by 150 men, and the operation took only two hours. Three months later all the chains were in place and the road platform was quickly completed. The bridge survived unaltered until the 1930s, when the present steel chains were installed.

RAILWAYS
Barmouth: Mawddach viaduct

This section of the Cambrian Coast line was opened in 1867, and the Mawddach viaduct, designed by Benjamin Piercy, was one of its most remarkable engineering works. It was not a sophisticated design, but considerable determination must have been needed to sink the five hundred timber piles necessary to support the 113 spans. The viaduct was extensively altered in the 1890s, when the present steel section, incorporating a swing-bridge, was introduced. The structure came close to being written off in the late 1970s when the piles were found to be dangerously eaten away by shipworms, but the decision was made to repair it. Some piles were replaced by tougher wood and the others were encased in cement.

Conwy: railway bridge

The construction of the railway along the North Wales coast necessitated the building of a new bridge (1848) alongside Telford's road bridge. Robert Stephenson used the fairly new technique, not hitherto seen in Britain, of running the track through long rigid box sections constructed of girders and iron plates. The bridge was used as a trial for the more difficult spanning of the Menai Strait (see below). The boxes were prefabricated, floated into position and raised by hydraulic lifts. Like Telford, the architect Francis Thompson tried to make the bridge towers harmonise with the castle.

Conwy Valley line

When the decision was made to extend the Conwy Valley branch line to Blaenau Ffestiniog (see chapter 9) there were considerable engineering difficulties caused by sharply rising ground, including a tunnel which became the longest in Wales. Its northern portal is at OS 115: SH 687504 and it ends close to Blaenau Ffestiniog station. Also noteworthy is the remote but very grand Gethin's Bridge at SH 782540.

Menai Strait: railway bridge

Like the Conwy railway bridge this was designed by Robert Stephenson in association with the architect Francis Thompson. Stephenson encountered the same Admiralty requirement for unobstructed headroom that

The Mawddach viaduct, Cambrian Coast railway.

had forced Telford into choosing a suspension bridge. Thus his first plan for a conventional two-arch cast iron bridge had to be abandoned. He substituted a scheme for box sections supported by suspension chains but was persuaded by a fellow engineer that the boxes would be sufficiently rigid and that suspension was unnecessary, in spite of the length of the spans. The final version required three stone towers to hold the boxes, which were built on the shore in eight sections (four per track) and raised from rafts by hydraulic lifts as at Conwy, although the operation was on a vastly bigger scale. The bridge was opened in 1850. In 1970 the tubes were destroyed by fire and were replaced by a steel-arched double-deck structure retaining the stone towers. At the same time provision was made for a second deck to carry a new road crossing.

MINING

See chapter 7 for reopened slate mines at Blaenau Ffestiniog and Harlech and the copper mine at Beddgelert. The exploration of disused mines is dangerous and not recommended for non-experts – they are in any case normally on private property. One exception is the following:

Parys Mountain, Anglesey. 2 miles (3 km) south of Amlwch.

This hill was excavated for copper in Roman times, but the discovery of a rich vein in the eighteenth century led to intensive exploitation. By 1780 more than 3000 tons of ore were being excavated each year and 1500 workers were employed – the biggest copper-mining operation in Europe. At this time ore was extracted by driving shafts into the hill, some of them below sea-level, but later the method changed to open-cast working. It is this that has produced the spectacular crater which can be seen today from public footpaths beginning at OS 114: SH 438907. Water was pumped out of the deep workings by machinery powered by a windmill, the tower of which still stands on top of the hill.

SLATE MINES AND QUARRIES

Until the second half of the eighteenth century slate was produced mainly by individuals or small groups operating under licence from the landowner. Increasing demand, which rose to a peak in the mid nineteenth century, led to the owners maximising production by forming their own companies and working on

an increasingly ambitious scale. As a result Gwynedd, and particularly the old county of Caernarfon, had Britain's biggest slate quarries at Bethesda, Llanberis and Nantlle and the most extensive slate mines at Blaenau Ffestiniog, as well as numerous workings elsewhere. Like abandoned mines, old quarries are dangerous, and unauthorised exploration is not permitted by the owners. Some of the largest workings, however, have been opened to the public and others can be viewed from public roads or paths.

Bethesda: Penrhyn slate quarries

Once claimed as the deepest hole in the world, these slate quarries are vast and impressive. They can be viewed to some extent from minor roads to the west of the village, and group tours (but not individual visits) are available by prior arrangement. The original quarries here were started in the mid eighteenth century by Richard Pennant, later Lord Penrhyn, who increased production from about 2000 tons in 1780 to 20,000 tons in 1800. In 1836 production rose to 80,000 tons, and the village of Bethesda was populated almost entirely by Penrhyn workers.

Blaenau Ffestiniog

Open-cast quarrying began here in the 1760s, but by the early nineteenth century it was becoming clear that the best slate lay deep within the hills, so mining operations began. Nowadays this grim process is vividly recreated at the Gloddfa Ganol and Llechwedd slate museums (chapter 7), which enable the visitor to experience the vast caverns that resulted.

Llanberis: Dinorwic slate quarries

These are best viewed from Llanberis itself, but the Welsh Slate Museum (see chapter 7) offers a closer view, with paths open to visitors (leaflets from the museum). The Dinorwic and Penrhyn quarries cut into opposite sides of the same mountain, Elidir Fawr. Work started at Llanberis in 1809 on the initiative of the landowner, Thomas Assheton Smith, and a hundred years later three thousand men were employed. Much use was made of tramway inclines to bring the slate down to the dressing floors, and increasing mechanisation during the nineteenth century led to the setting up of centralised workshops for its maintenance. These buildings, of some architectural merit, still stand and now house the Welsh Slate

The slate workings loom over Blaenau Ffestiniog.

Museum. Another major feature was the railway which carried the slates to Port Dinorwic on the Menai Strait (see chapter 9).

Nantlle slate quarries

The B4418 from Rhydd-Ddu (OS 115: SH 569534) passes through this less well known but very dramatic area, providing views of the old quarries, which are not open to the public. The most famous working was the Dorothea, a vast hole created by starting quarrying at the top of the hill and working downwards. The slate was taken away by a railway running down the Llyfni valley to Penygroes and then on to the 'slate quay' at Caernarfon (now occupied by the main car park).

Ystradllyn slate works.
North-west of Porthmadog. OS 124: SH 549434.

Extensive remains survive of this mill, which was designed to process slate from the Gorseddau quarries beyond the reservoir to the north-east. It was driven by water power by means of an aqueduct from the river. The trackbed of the railway which connected the quarries with Porthmadog is marked on the Ordnance Survey map and can still be followed for some distance as a public footpath.

43

STONE QUARRIES

Gwynedd's hard igneous rock was much in demand in the nineteenth century, both for building construction and in the form of 'granite setts' for paving city streets. The majority of quarries were on the coast and made use of specially built shipping piers to take the stone away.

Penmaenmawr

Stone from here was used extensively by Thomas Telford in making the Chester-Holyhead road, but production did not peak until the 1920s. It is still a major source of roadstone. Operations over more than 150 years have left dramatic scars on the hills behind the town.

Trefor, Lleyn peninsula. 6 miles (10 km) north-east of Nefyn.

There are extensive granite quarries above the village and the jetty is still in place. From here ships transported granite paving blocks to the towns and cities of north-west England. A public footpath clearly marked on the Ordnance Survey map leads from Trefor to Llithfaen and passes close to the quarry area.

WINDMILLS

Anglesey was once noted for its windmills. Towers can be seen near **Amlwch** at OS 114: SH 440923, at **Brynteg** (SH 496829) and on top of **Parys Mountain** (SH 445095). The best preserved example is at **Llanddeusant** (SH 340854).

Anglesey's only working windmill at Llanddeusant.

The Ffestiniog Railway, Porthmadog.

9
Railways

Railways have played a vital part in the economy of Gwynedd, whether in the form of industrial tracks that brought out slate, stone and other minerals from remote sites or as a means of encouraging the early holiday trade. The majority of Wales's famous restored narrow-gauge lines are in Gwynedd, and in recent years British Rail has begun to appreciate the tourist value of some lines that were once threatened with closure. In addition to the obvious attractions of the restored railways, it is worth investigating BR's 'package deals' in North Wales. (Railway features of interest to enthusiasts are described in chapter 8.)

BRITISH RAIL SERVICES
Cambrian Coast Line. Machynlleth to Pwllheli.

Early main-line railways in Wales were routed along the coasts because of the formidable engineering problems involved in crossing the high country inland. In the mid nineteenth century several grandiose schemes were proposed for lines through the middle of Wales that would connect the west coast with

the English Midlands and open it up to holidaymakers. There were plans too for alternative Irish ferry ports. In 1853 the famous entrepreneur David Davies won the contract for a line from Newtown along the Severn valley to Llanidloes. It was completed in 1859, and very soon afterwards a line from Newtown to Oswestry provided a link with the English railway system. Another contractor, Thomas Savin, began work on a line from Machynlleth to Aberystwyth, while Davies undertook the thankless task of connecting Llanidloes with Machynlleth, which involved excavating a 120 foot (37 metre) cutting through the mountains at Talerddig (at the time the deepest cutting in the world). The whole line was finally completed in 1864 and was taken over almost immediately by the newly formed Cambrian Railways Company, which continued the line up the coast and round to Pwllheli, a project involving the building of a notable viaduct across the Mawddach estuary at Barmouth (see chapter 8).

The line revolutionised the economy of the west coast, creating prosperous resorts at

Trains on the Llanberis Lake Railway.

Aberystwyth, Tywyn, Barmouth, Criccieth and Pwllheli, and providing industrial outlets at Tywyn and Porthmadog. In spite of occasional closure threats the line has survived, and 'station-hopping' along the section between Tywyn and Pwllheli has become a popular holiday activity. Apart from the scenic value, the stations give easy access both to the sea and to the hills, and there are connections with narrow-gauge lines at Barmouth, Tywyn and Porthmadog.

Chester to Holyhead line

Opened in 1850 by the London and North-Western Railway, this line provided North Wales with its first rail link to London. At the height of operations about twelve thousand men were working on the line, and construction involved some remarkable engineering achievements, such as the 700 yard (640 metre) tunnel at the notorious Penmaenmawr headland and the pioneering tubular bridges by Robert Stephenson at Conwy and the Menai Strait (see chapter 8). As soon as the line was completed to Bangor every effort was made to attract visitors to the North Wales coast, beginning a process which has made it one of Britain's most popular holiday areas. The line's most famous train, the Irish Mail, was

inaugurated in 1860, taking 6¹/₂ hours to travel from London to Holyhead. Today's trains are not so glamorous, although steam-hauled trains have been revived on the line on certain days during the summer months. A special ticket offering a day's unlimited travel on this and the Conwy Valley line is available.

Conwy Valley line. Llandudno to Blaenau Ffestiniog.

This is another line that has survived against the odds. The original plan of 1846 was for a line running direct from Conwy along the west bank to the busy market town of Llanrwst. This was later changed to a proposal for an east-bank route, linking with the Chester-Holyhead line at a new station called Llandudno Junction, already built to provide a branch line to Llandudno. The line was started in 1860 and reached Llanrwst in 1863, when the tourist potential of Betws-y-coed encouraged an extension to the village. This led the quarry owners at Blaenau Ffestiniog to seek a further extension up the Penmachno valley to provide a quicker outlet for their slates, although their enthusiasm for the project lessened when steam was introduced on the Ffestiniog Railway (see below). Despite having no guarantee of slate traffic the LNWR proceeded to start a line between Betws-y-coed and Blaenau Ffestiniog in 1872, boring the longest tunnel in Wales with enormous difficulty and many casualties. The line was completed in 1879 and was seldom economic. Threatened with closure in 1968, it was reprieved to assist with the building of Trawsfynydd nuclear power station, while a limited passenger service was maintained. Eventually its value to tourism was realised and the very scenic line was revived to connect with the narrow-gauge Ffestiniog Railway. The Conwy Valley line is included in the special day ticket for the Chester-Holyhead line mentioned above, but there is also a separate day ticket for unlimited travel. A day spent on the line can be very rewarding, with several attractions around Llanrwst, walks from Betws-y-coed, the reopened mines at Blaenau Ffestiniog and the chance to travel down to Porthmadog on the Ffestiniog Railway.

NARROW-GAUGE LINES

Bala Lake Railway, The Station, Llanuwchllyn, Bala LL23 7DD. Telephone: 06784 666.

The narrow-gauge line is unusual in having been laid on the trackbed of the former GWR standard-gauge line from Ruabon to Barmouth, which was closed in 1965. The first train ran in 1972, and small steam locomotives which once worked in the slate quarries of North Wales now haul the trains. The 2 foot (610 mm) gauge track provides a 9 mile (14 km) return journey of about one hour between Llanuwchllyn and Bala beside Llyn Tegid, the largest natural lake in Wales. Engines and rolling stock are on view at Llanuwchllyn, where there is also a cafe and souvenir shop.

Fairbourne Railway, Fairbourne, Gwynedd LL38 2PZ. Telephone: 0341 250362.

Opened over a hundred years ago, originally as a horse-drawn tramway, by Mr McDougall of self-raising flour fame, the Fairbourne Railway was completely rebuilt in 1986. It has five charming steam locomotives of $12\frac{1}{2}$ inch (311 mm) gauge and vintage coaches. The line runs by the sea and affords fine views of the Mawddach estuary and surrounding mountains. It can be reached from Fairbourne or by ferry from Barmouth. Other attractions include an ornamental fowl reserve, restaurant and craft shop.

Ffestiniog Railway, Porthmadog LL49 9NF. Telephone: 0766 512340.

The Ffestiniog Railway opened in 1836 to carry slate from Blaenau Ffestiniog to the new harbour at Porthmadog. Horses would draw the empty wagons up the 14 mile (22 km) route and be carried in the back of the train on the downward journey, which relied on gravity.

The Talyllyn Railway: locomotive number 1, 'Talyllyn', at Nant Gwernol station.

CHAPTER 9

Steam locomotives were first used in 1863, and their success led to a passenger service being started two years later. The railway was noted for pioneering the Fairlie double-boilered engine that was later adopted all over the world for work in difficult and steep terrain. The line was abandoned in 1946, but in 1954 volunteers began work on its restoration, and by 1978 the line had been extended in stages to reach Tanygrisiau. Here the new power station created difficulties, and the company embarked on a major engineering project to re-route the track in order to reach Blaenau Ffestiniog.

Today the Ffestiniog line twists and loops its way for 13^1/$_2$ miles (22 km) up into the hills to reach Blaenau Ffestiniog, where it connects with British Rail's Conwy Valley line to Llandudno. It is a two-hour round trip. Refreshments are available on the train and at Porthmadog station, and also at Tan-y-Bwlch station in the summer, and there is a souvenir shop.

Llanberis Lake Railway, Llanberis, Caernarfon LL55 4TY. Telephone: 0286 870549.

This railway has a long ancestry. The first track along Llyn Padarn was laid in the 1820s as a horse tramway carrying slate from the Dinorwic quarries to Port Dinorwic on the Menai Strait. Steam power was introduced in 1848, and one of the original locomotives is on show at Penrhyn Castle (see chapter 6). The railway closed in 1961, and the lines at the quarry itself were abandoned in 1967, but local enthusiasts revived it in 1971 by laying a new line along a stretch of the old trackbed and bringing back into service three late nineteenth-century Hunslet locomotives. The line now runs beside Llyn Padarn from Gilfach Ddu station at the Welsh Slate Museum (see chapter 7) to Penllyn, a round trip of about forty minutes. There is a cafeteria service.

Snowdon Mountain Railway, Llanberis, Caernarfon LL55 4TY. Telephone: 0286 870223.

Since 1896 steam engines have been pushing carriages up the only public rack railway in Britain to the summit of Snowdon, and seven of the original Swiss-built locomotives are still in use, together with two British-built diesels. Visitors should note that trains do not run to a strict timetable: services may be cancelled or shortened in the event of strong winds or other adverse weather, and most

trains will not start without at least 25 passengers aboard. The journey takes one hour each way, and there is a half-hour stay on the summit, where a cafe is normally open. 59 passengers can travel on each train and trains normally run at half-hour intervals in the peak season. There are often queues in the summer but leaflets available locally give details of a form of reservation service. Passengers travelling up are entitled to a seat on the same train going down, so it is rarely possible in the summer to walk to the summit and catch a train back.

Talyllyn Railway, Wharf Station, Tywyn LL36 9EY. Telephone: 0654 710472.

The Talyllyn was the first railway in Britain to be restored to operation by volunteers and claims an unbroken record of service since 1865, when it was opened to carry passengers and slates from Abergynolwyn to Tywyn, a distance of 7 miles (11 km). The major engineering achievement was the Dolgoch viaduct, 52 feet (16 metres) high. The line survived precariously until after the Second World War, when it was still using its original locomotives and rolling stock. It escaped nationalisation, but after the death of the owner in 1950 it seemed doomed until the first group of railway preservationists in Britain took over its management.

The line runs through high and romantic countryside to a terminus near Abergynolwyn, where there are several waymarked forest walks. The round trip takes about two hours and there are refreshment facilities at each end. A narrow-gauge railway museum has been set up at Tywyn.

Welsh Highland Railway, Tremadog Road, Porthmadog. Telephone enquiries: 0248 671232.

Planned in 1872 as part of an ambitious scheme to link Caernarfon with Betws-y-coed, Beddgelert, Porthmadog and Corwen, the Welsh Highland was a notoriously unreliable railway and always financially insecure. It struggled on until 1937 and was then abandoned (part of its trackbed forms a popular walk from Beddgelert). A short length of track has been relaid by enthusiasts at Porthmadog and offers a short run of about a mile (1.6 km) each way at the time of writing, though the track is being extended. A mixture of steam and diesel locomotives is used. There is a cafe and a large railway bookshop.

Portmeirion.

10
Other attractions

Anglesey Bird World, Tynparc, Dwyran, Llanfairpwll LL61 6RP. Telephone: 0248 79627.

Exotic birds, waterfowl and poultry are on display, together with sheep, goats and pets in their own compound. Refreshments are available and there is a children's play area with a hand-propelled go-kart track.

Anglesey Sea Zoo, Brynsiencyn, Anglesey LL61 6TQ. Telephone: 0248 430411.

The zoo is a sophisticated marine aquarium with an extensive collection of fish and other sea creatures imaginatively displayed. The complex is completely under cover. Other attractions include a children's adventure trail, model boats, water games, a seafood bar and a restaurant.

Butterfly Palace (Pili Palas), Ffordd Penmynydd, Menai Bridge LL59 5RP. Telephone: 0248 712474.

A wide range of exhibits is featured, including butterflies in a tropical environment, tropical birds, reptiles and exotic insects. There is a pets' corner and adventure playground, a shop and a cafe.

Cae Du Farm Park, Beddgelert LL55 4NE. Telephone: 076686 345.

This is a 300 acre (121 ha) working farm with a 1½ mile (2.4 km) trail, much of it beside the river Glaslyn, that takes in not only routine farming operations but a wide range of rare breeds and wildfowl.

Centre for Alternative Technology, Machynlleth, Powys SY20 9AZ. Telephone: 0654 702400. Off A487, 2½ miles (4 km) north of Machynlleth.

The centre was set up in an old slate quarry in the early 1970s as an experiment in living with alternative forms of energy. Since then the community has expanded its activities, and the site abounds in interesting displays of solar and wind power, low-energy dwellings, self-build houses, organic farming and gardening and many other 'green' projects. There is a children's playground, an excellent bookshop and a restaurant.

Conwy Butterfly House, Bodlondeb Park, Conwy LL32 8DU. Telephone: 0492 593149.

Tropical butterflies fly freely in a jungle environment.

CHAPTER 10

Ffestiniog Pumped Storage Power Station,
Tanygrisiau, Blaenau Ffestiniog LL41 3TP. Telephone: 0766 830310.

The power station is of the hydro-electric pumped storage type, whereby water from an upper dam is released through the turbines to generate electricity when needed and pumped back up when demand for electricity is lighter. The power station is set in a dramatic landscape close to the Blaenau Ffestiniog slate quarries. There are hourly guided tours in the summer and visitors can travel to the spectacular site of the upper dam. Other facilities include an exhibition, souvenir shop and cafe.

Hen Blas Country Park and Adventureland,
Bodorgan, Anglesey LL62 5DL. Telephone: 0407 840152. Off B4422, 3 miles (5 km) south-west of Llangefni.

Hen Blas is a centre for family entertainment including a seventeenth-century manor house and gardens, an audio-visual interpretation of local history, a Shire horse centre, falconry display, working smithy and many other attractions.

Inigo Jones, Tudor Slate Works, Groeslon,
near Caernarfon LL54 7ST. Telephone: 0286 830242. Off A487 between Groeslon and Pen-y-Groes.

This is a rare example of an operational slate works. The firm manufactures various articles from slate, and visitors can follow all stages of production from the raw slate to finished work, including engraving. The tour is self-guided, and a souvenir booklet is provided. Facilities include a showroom, video and audio taped commentary, and cafe.

Above: *A wind generator at the Centre for Alternative Technology, Machynlleth.*

Right: *A craftsman at work at Inigo Jones.*

The Victorian pump room at Trefriw Spa, now in operation again.

Meirion Mill, Dinas Mawddwy, Machynlleth, Powys SY20 9LS. Telephone: 06504 311.

The large mill shop sells quality woollens, crafts and gifts, and there is a restaurant and coffee shop. See also Dinas Mawddwy in chapter 12.

Portmeirion, near Porthmadog LL48 6ET. Telephone: 0766 770228.

Portmeirion lies on a rocky headland between the estuaries of the rivers Glaslyn and Dwyryd. In 1926 the distinguished architect Sir Clough Williams-Ellis bought the estate and set out to transform it into an exotic Italianate village. The original mansion was transformed into a hotel, and other buildings were either constructed from scratch or brought here from elsewhere and rebuilt (several examples of fine architecture and design have been saved in this way). Skilfully contrived vistas add to the visual appeal. The village is set in woodland and subtropical gardens with fine views over the sea, and there are shops, a hotel and self-service restaurant; an audio-visual presentation tells the story of the village.

The Time Tunnel, The Green, Beaumaris. Telephone: 0248 810072.

The Time Tunnel is a sound and light presentation of the history of human endeavour in North Wales from prehistoric times, together with a reconstruction of life on an emigrant ship. Additional facilities include children's entertainments and a cafe.

Trefriw Wells Spa, Trefriw, Llanrwst LL27 0JS. Telephone: 0492 640057.

The spa, very popular in the nineteenth century, has been revived. Guided tours take in the caves where the spring rises, the Victorian bath-house, a unique 'Cyclopean' bath-house and the original bottling plant. Medicinal spa water, licensed as a medicine in Germany, can be purchased and there is a cafe and a souvenir shop.

Trefriw Woollen Mills, Trefriw, Llanrwst LL27 0NQ. Telephone: 0492 640462.

The mills are powered by water turbines. Visitors can see the weaving and tour the mill which manufactures tweeds and bedspreads from the raw wool. There are also handspinning demonstrations in summer, a shop and a cafe.

Welsh Mountain Zoo and Gardens, Old Highway, Colwyn Bay, Clwyd LL28 5UY. Telephone: 0492 532938. Off B5113, west of town centre.

The zoo is not in Gwynedd but it is a well established North Wales attraction owned by the Zoological Society of Wales. In addition to the wide range of animals in natural settings, the site itself is splendidly situated and includes landscaped gardens and woodland, providing pleasant walks and an adventure trail for children.

Wylfa Nuclear Power Station, Cemaes Bay, Anglesey LL67 0DH. Telephone: 0407 710471.

Wylfa is the largest and most advanced power station of its type in the world, with two Magnox reactors. Guided tours are available, and the information centre contains a souvenir shop, cinema and exhibition.

Cadair Idris, above Dolgellau.

11
The mountains

Serious climbers and mountain-walking specialists have their own guides to Gwynedd, and the following notes are for the benefit of the ordinary visitor wishing to experience the mountains at close quarters without undue risk. However, there is no reason why an active family should not attempt some of the mountain walks, and the National Park Authority has made available at information centres a series of leaflets with maps and directions for a wide range of routes. For walking of any kind in Snowdonia there is no substitute for the Ordnance Survey's large-scale Outdoor Leisure maps.

The often repeated warnings about suitable clothing and footwear and proficiency in map and compass reading definitely apply in these mountains. The danger on popular paths is minimal in good clear weather, but the experience of being suddenly enclosed in mist is frightening and disorientating. It is essential that anyone embarking on a long walk should notify someone of the route and the estimated time of return.

The Arans
This range rises at the western end of Llyn Tegid (Bala Lake) and continues southwards to Dinas Mawddwy, reaching its maximum height at a ridge with two peaks, Aran Fawddwy and Aran Benllyn. Surprisingly Aran Fawddwy, at 2975 feet (907 metres), is the highest mountain in Wales south of Snowdon. The range forms a very empty landscape with few public paths, although certain 'courtesy paths' have been designated by the landowner and are shown on a map issued by the National Park Authority. In any case the remoter areas are dangerous territory for inexperienced walkers.

One way of sampling the mountains by car is to take the minor road from Dinas Mawddwy to Lake Vyrnwy over Bwlch-y-groes; it is not a trip for those of nervous disposition and not a road on which to break down – outside the summer months it can be deserted for long periods. Another good route is up the Cywarch valley by a lane which branches off the Lake Vyrnwy road just outside Dinas Mawddwy (OS 125: SH 868158) and reaches a point beneath Craig Cywarch. This is a popular climbing crag, so a footpath leads to it from the top of the lane.

The Arenigs
Arenig Fawr and Arenig Fach rise prominently on each side of the A4212 Bala-Trawsfynydd road just west of Llyn Celyn.

There is no easy way of exploring them, although Arenig Fawr, to the south, is a feasible climb for the moderately fit (consult the National Park literature for the designated path). On its summit is a memorial to the crew of a United States Air Force plane which crashed into the mountain during the Second World War.

Cadair Idris

Cadair Idris is not a mountain but a long craggy escarpment to the south of Dolgellau, 4 miles (6 km) in length and rising to its highest point at Penygadair (2928 feet or 893 metres), which is roughly at the centre. Mynydd Moel forms a secondary peak to the east. From Penygadair another ridge runs south and turns to enclose Llyn Cau. There are various routes on to Cadair Idris, but for the inexperienced walker the choice lies between the path starting by a parking place near Llyn Gwernan on the northern side (OS 124: SH 698153) and a route beginning near Tal-y-llyn lake to the south at OS 124: SH 730114. The large-scale Ordnance Survey Outdoor Leisure map should be used for the ascent since it marks the paths with much greater clarity. The ridges provide enough fine walking without the need to reach Penygadair itself, though there is no doubt that the walk along the escarpment to Mynydd Moel is very satisfying.

The Llanberis pass.

The Carneddau

This large expanse of rounded mountains forms a rough triangle in northern Snowdonia bounded by the Conwy valley, the Conwy-Bangor coast and the Nant Ffrancon pass. There are seven summits at over 3000 feet (915 metres) in the range, including Carnedd Llewelyn and Carnedd Dafydd, respectively the second and third highest summits in Wales. Rising virtually straight from the sea at some points along the northern coast (notoriously at Penmaenmawr), they were an obstacle to east-west communications for centuries, and the modern north coast road and railway are forced through tunnels. The Romans established a marching route through the Bwlch-y-Ddeufaen pass further south, but it was not until the early nineteenth century that Thomas Telford engineered an easy coach road by way of the Nant Ffrancon pass (see chapter 8).

These are the remotest mountains in Wales – not an area for solitary walking and no place to be if a mist descends because most paths are indistinct. The safest way for the average visitor to experience the range on foot is to follow the old Roman road, starting at the village of Roewen (OS 115: SH 756720). It is an easy walk to Bwlch-y-Ddeufaen, and the track continues to the coast at Aber. At the entrance to Gwern gof Isaf farm on the A5 west of Capel Curig (OS 115: SH 685600) there is

a National Trust map showing short local walks into the Carneddau. Cars can be left here. (See chapter 5 for interesting churches in the hills to the west of the Conwy valley.)

The Glyders

The Glyder group lies between the Nant Ffrancon and Llanberis passes, and their highest points form an intermittent curving ridge that starts to the west of Capel Curig and peters out on the approach to Bethesda (the A5 follows its line). The highest points on the ridge, from east to west, are Glyder Fach (3262 feet or 994 metres), Glyder Fawr (3279 feet or 999 metres) and Y Garn (3104 feet or 946 metres), and above Llanberis the much quarried Elidir Fawr stands at 3030 feet or 924 metres. However, the most famous, because the most obvious, is Tryfan (3010 feet or 917 metres), which looms starkly beside the A5 above Llyn Ogwen. The Glyders are definitely for fit and properly equipped walkers, although the casual visitor can experience their grandeur from a lower level by walking the Cwm Idwal nature trail (see chapter 2).

The Rhinogs

This 14 mile (22 km) expanse of high moorland with rocky outcrops extends from the Mawddach valley to the Ffestiniog valley, rising to a height of 2475 feet (756 metres) at Yr Lethr. It is one of the most desolate areas of Wales, notable for its many prehistoric sites (some of them described in chapter 3) and for its ancient trackways leading from the coast across to Bala. The Outdoor Leisure map shows the major tracks, which can still be followed by the enthusiast, and the motorised visitor can share the experience quite easily by taking the road from Llanbedr (3 miles or 5 km south of Harlech) up to the fine lake at Cwm Bychan. Various paths start here, the most famous being the so-called 'Roman Steps' (probably laid as part of the medieval packhorse route), which provide an exhilarating walk on a fine day.

Tryfan, Snowdonia's most popular mountain for climbing and scrambling.

Snowdon from Glaslyn valley.

Siabod and the Moelwyns

Moel Siabod is the stark peak that looms to the south of Capel Curig. Beyond it a forbidding range extends south-westwards to Blaenau Ffestiniog, where Moelwyn Mawr rises to 2527 feet (770 metres). This is inhospitable country for the casual visitor, although the long ridge of Cnicht, to the north-west of Moelwyn Mawr, is a popular objective for walkers and can be climbed by properly clothed and shod non-experts by way of a path starting at the old quarrying village of Croesor (OS 115: SH 630446).

The Snowdon massif

The massif is bounded to the north by the A4086 through the Llanberis pass, to the east by the A498 through the Nantgwynant pass and to the south by the A4085 from Beddgelert to Caernarfon. Snowdon itself, at 3560 feet (1085 metres), is not a solitary and dramatic peak and can be surprisingly difficult to identify. It is the centre and culmination of a series of ridges which offer fine opportunities for experienced walkers but which should be avoided by anyone else.

Paradoxically, Snowdon itself is the most accessible of mountains. Thousands who climb it each year are disappointed at finding the views obscured by mist, but on the right day the experience can be spectacular. Apart from the railway (see chapter 9) there are well established paths to the summit, demanding varying degrees of fitness. They are described in leaflets obtainable locally. The simplest and safest, but dullest, follows the railway line. The Pyg Track and Miners' Track start from a car park at Pen-y-pass, at the top of the Llanberis pass. In the summer parking space cannot be relied on, and easily the best plan is to leave the car in Llanberis and take a Sherpa bus to Pen-y-pass (there is a regular service in both directions). A route worth considering (it is reasonably easy and likely to be less crowded) is the path which ascends from the car park at Rhyd-Ddu, on the A4085 north of Beddgelert. A descent is then possible by the Snowdon Ranger path, which returns to a point just under 2 miles (3 km) from Rhyd-Ddu.

All the paths are well beaten, but be prepared for a big temperature difference at the top, and carry food and drink – do not rely on finding the summit cafe open.

The harbour at Barmouth.

12
Towns and villages

ABERDARON

This is a very attractive harbour village on the end of the Lleyn peninsula, with steep and narrow streets and a long sandy beach. It was the final staging post for medieval pilgrims before they embarked on the dangerous crossing to Bardsey Island. The cafe called Y Gegin Fawr is thought to have been a pilgrims' rest house in the fourteenth century. The island can be viewed by taking the fine cliff walk to the west. (See chapter 5 for the church.)

Although **Bardsey Island** lies close to the end of the Lleyn peninsula it has always been difficult to reach because of the fierce currents in Bardsey Sound. This isolation made it an ideal place for a Celtic monastery, and the earliest religious foundation was established

in AD 615. The tradition that it was the burial place of twenty thousand saints made it a powerful attraction for medieval pilgrims. Nowadays the only religious survival is a section of the thirteenth-century abbey tower. In more recent years the island has been farmed, but it is now best known for its bird observatory. The island is not normally open to the public.

ABERDYFI

Aberdyfi (Aberdovey) is a pleasant straggling village with long terraces of Victorian houses, lying under hills beside the Dyfi estuary. Once a small commercial port, it is now a popular centre for sailing and water sports, and in addition it has 5 miles (8 km) of sandy beach. On the other side of the estuary, in Dyfed, are the nature reserves of Ynyslas and Ynyshir.

ABERFFRAW

This small village on the south coast of Anglesey once enjoyed considerable prestige as the seat of the Princes of North Wales between the ninth and thirteenth centuries. It has a sixteenth-century packhorse bridge and a church of some interest. Extensive sand dunes lie to the east. (See chapter 3 for Barclodiad-y-Gawres.)

ABERSOCH

This is a favourite sailing and holiday centre on the southern coast of the Lleyn peninsula, with sandy beaches and an attractive harbour. A road to the south leads on to the headland of Trwyn Cilan, overlooking the 4 mile (6 km) expanse of empty sand called Porth Neigwl. Its other name is Hell's Mouth, a reminder of the number of sailing ships beached here through a combination of high winds and dangerous currents. On the eastern side of the headland the two St Tudwal's Islands can be seen. On one of them are the ruins of a chapel which may have belonged to a small religious community set up at the place where the saint had his cell. The islands are not open to the public. (See chapter 5 for Capel Newydd and Llanengan church.)

AMLWCH

This former commercial port on the north coast of Anglesey grew up to serve the copper-mining area of Parys Mountain to the west. In the early nineteenth century it is reputed to have had over a thousand alehouses to serve its population of six thousand. It lost its importance with the decline of the copper industry but in recent times has gained an oil terminal and a chemical works. There is an excellent leisure centre and good coastal walking around Bull Bay. (See chapter 8 for Parys Mountain.)

BALA

Early closing Wednesday; market day Thursday.

Bala is a small market town that has retained its character in spite of its summer invasion by visitors, attracted by its position at the head of Llyn Tegid, the largest natural lake in Wales and a popular sailing centre. The town lies on an old Roman road, adopted in the Norman grid plan – hence the long straight main street,

lined with pubs, useful shops and eating places. There is a castle motte in the town centre but otherwise Bala shows few signs of its medieval origins, and its character is homely Victorian.

It has played its part in Welsh history. A statue in the main street commemorates Thomas Edward Ellis, a forceful campaigner for Welsh nationalism in the late nineteenth century, and another statue in Tegid Street is a reminder that this was the adopted town of Thomas Charles (1755-1814), the great Methodist preacher and religious reformer. Charles's grandson was partly responsible for the building in 1837 of the Calvinistic Methodist College, which still stands beside the A4212 on the outskirts of the town. Another Bala minister, Michael Jones, was influential in the founding of the famous Welsh colony in Patagonia.

The B4391 to the south-east is a popular drive, passing over bleak high moorland to the old mining and quarrying village of **Llangynog**, before which there are spectacular views of the Tanat valley. (See chapter 9 for Bala Lake Railway, which is the best way to travel the length of the lake.)

BANGOR

Early closing Wednesday; market day Friday.

In recent years Bangor has become a much more tranquil town, following the construction of the A55 to the south, which acts as a bypass for the Holyhead traffic. Established in AD 564 by St Deiniol, Bangor is the oldest diocese in England and Wales, and when the University College was founded in 1883 it became the undisputed cultural capital of North Wales. It nevertheless remains a modest town with a Georgian and Victorian personality best appreciated among the buildings lining its pedestrianised High Street. The University has now spread considerably since its original Jacobean-style buildings were opened in 1911, not long after the major restoration of the Cathedral, which is now rather disappointing architecturally. The city shows a different face along its waterfront. Before Thomas Telford bridged the Menai Strait Bangor was not only a major staging point on the Holyhead road but a busy port; the harbour area has now regained much of its life as a sailing centre, and the restored pier adds a cheerful touch. On the A487 south-west of the town is **Port Dinorwic**, created in the early nineteenth century as an outlet for slates from the quarries at

Llewelyn Cottage, Beddgelert.

Llanberis (the quarry owner lived nearby at Vaynol Hall). (See chapter 5 for the Cathedral, chapter 6 for Penrhyn Castle and chapter 7 for the Museum and Art Gallery.)

BARMOUTH
Early closing Wednesday; market day Thursday.

Barmouth grew up as a small port, and its centre still has the feeling of a harbour, with much sailing activity and buildings perched on the hills behind. Its modern growth, however, started with the arrival of the railway, when its potential as a seaside resort was heavily promoted. Its big church, well worth visiting, dates from this time, and so do many of the larger houses and hotels, which offer some interesting Victorian architecture. Apart from its sandy beaches, much of its appeal lay in the hills above it, and this remains true today. The famous viewpoint of Dinas Olau stands above the town – the first acquisition by the National Trust in 1885. There are several long-established hill walks, including the famous Panorama Walk, and it is possible to cross the estuary or admire the views from the pedestrian tollbridge beside the railway viaduct. (See chapter 3 for Dyffryn Ardudwy

burial chambers, chapter 8 for the railway bridge and chapter 9 for the Fairbourne Railway.)

BEAUMARIS

Several large inns mark out Beaumaris as a place of some consequence. Before the Menai Strait was bridged it was not only the main port for Anglesey but the administrative centre too, and the legacy is a cheerful waterfront full of pleasure craft and streets lined with handsome buildings – a pleasant place to wander in. The parish church is worth visiting for its late fifteenth-century chancel, which contains carved stalls with misericords and an impressive alabaster tomb of the same period. (See chapter 4 for the castle and Penmon Priory, chapter 7 for the Museum of Childhood and the Gaol and Courthouse, and chapter 10 for the Time Tunnel.)

BEDDGELERT

A small grey village in the heart of the mountains, Beddgelert stands at the confluence of two rivers, and its old bridge is its focal point. Thousands of visitors each year walk to the grave of the dog Gelert (the story is inscribed on a board near the bridge) although the 'legend' was long ago exposed as a Victorian publicity stunt. It indicates that Beddgelert developed early as a tourist attraction and it continues to do so, but the village is also a good walking centre. One popular short route is along the trackbed of the old Welsh Highland Railway to Nantmor. (See chapter 7 for Sygun Copper Mine and chapter 10 for Cae Du Farm Park.)

BETHESDA
Early closing Wednesday.

Lying at the foot of the Nant Ffrancon pass, Bethesda once housed thousands of workers at the vast Penrhyn slate quarries that loom behind the village (best seen from the elevated car park). Its name derives from its big central chapel, one of several in the town. Bethesda suffers from having the A5 as its High Street and has never become a tourist attraction, although devotees of Victorian architecture will find much of interest here. Slate is still produced at the quarries, reputed to be the deepest in Britain, and group visits are possible by arrangement (see chapter 8).

Above: *Gelert's grave, Beddgelert.*

Below: *Bethesda, with the Penrhyn quarries in the background.*

The church and green, Betws-y-coed.

BETWS-Y-COED
Early closing Thursday.

Idyllically situated amid forested mountains at the confluence of three rivers, Betws-y-coed was an important staging point on the Holyhead road – the easing of the formidable gradients between here and Capel Curig was one of Thomas Telford's more notable achievements. Later the village became a romantic resort for Victorian visitors, which accounts for the big nineteenth-century houses

lining its main street. (The famous and over-rated 'Swallow Falls' to the west of the town were exploited for profit at an early date.) Betws-y-coed has unashamedly devoted itself to the tourist industry ever since. Both the original village church (behind the station) and the big Victorian one deserve attention; the former contains the grave slab of Gruffudd, great-nephew of Prince Llewelyn the Last. The information centre gives details of the attractions here, including railway and motor

The slate fountain at Blaenau Ffestiniog.

museums and several good forest walks. The village station is on British Rail's enjoyable Conwy Valley line (chapter 9). (See chapter 3 for Capel Garmon burial chamber, chapter 4 for Dolwyddelan Castle, chapter 5 for Dolwyddelan church, chapter 6 for Ty Mawr Wybrnant, chapter 7 for the museums and chapter 8 for the Waterloo Bridge.)

BLAENAU FFESTINIOG
Early closing Thursday.

This straggling village developed out of the slate industry boom of the later nineteenth century. In its heyday it must have been a grim place to live, on an exposed mountainside and overshadowed by immense quarries. The town trail, available locally, is the best way of discovering its past, and some idea of the hardship involved in slate production can be gained by visiting the two reopened quarries. The Ffestiniog narrow-gauge railway terminates here and links with British Rail's line to Llandudno. (See chapter 7 for the Gloddfa Ganol and Llechwedd slate museums, chapter 9 for the Ffestiniog Railway and chapter 10 for the nearby Tanygrisiau power station.)

'Britain's Smallest House', Conwy, built into the thirteenth-century town wall.

BORTH-Y-GEST
This seaside village immediately south-west of Porthmadog is popular for family holidays and beach excursions.

CAERNARFON
Early closing Thursday; market day Friday.

In the thirteenth century Caernarfon achieved considerable status as the centre of English rule in North Wales (it is still the county town of Gwynedd) but much of its later prosperity was due to its harbour and its market. It is still an important commercial centre, but its wider fame derives from the castle, the scene of the investitures of two Princes of Wales in modern times. It is also popular as a sailing centre, as the crowded harbour testifies. The town centre is Castle Square (or Y Maes), with its pleasant mixture of architecture, and the narrow shopping streets are tucked away in the area originally enclosed by the walls extending from the castle. (See chapter 3 for Segontium Roman fort, chapter 4 for the castle, chapter 7 for the air and maritime museums and chapter 10 for Inigo Jones slate works.)

CAPEL CURIG
The Victorian popularity of Betws-y-coed soon spread along the Holyhead road to Capel Curig, and hotels of the period feature among the buildings straggling beside the A5, which rises to reach the village 'centre', at the junction of two busy Snowdonia roads and overshadowed by the peak of Moel Siabod. It is much frequented by walkers, climbers and other outdoor pursuits enthusiasts.

CEMAES
Cemaes, on the north coast of Anglesey, was a major port until superseded by its neighbour Amlwch during the great copper boom of the eighteenth and nineteenth centuries (see Amlwch, above). Today this attractive little harbour village draws holidaymakers to its beach and to the cliff walks on National Trust land to the east. (See chapter 2 for Cemlyn Bay nature reserve.)

CONWY
Early closing Wednesday; market days Tuesday (summer), Saturday (winter).

Conwy is unique in Wales in having more than a mile (1.6 km) of its thirteenth-century walls still standing. They compress the town centre into a grid of narrow intimate streets that have been notorious for traffic congestion in the past but which should be transformed when the town is finally bypassed. The walls are part of a defensive scheme that included Edward I's magnificent castle, the major

The harbour, Conwy.

attraction for visitors. Conwy's historical importance as a river crossing point is illustrated by the sight of Thomas Telford's elegantly castellated suspension bridge, Robert Stephenson's less elegant railway bridge and the massive modern road bridge, side by side beneath the castle. The harbour has lost most of its commercial vitality but it remains popular with sailing and fishing enthusiasts and is an attractive asset. The church should be visited for its splendid rood screen of about 1500 and its interesting tombs and memorials. Another famous attraction on the small quayside is 'Britain's Smallest House', set against the town wall. (See chapter 3 for Canovium Roman fort and Pen-y-Gaer hillfort, chapter 4 for the castle, chapter 5 for Llangelynnin Old Church, chapter 6 for Plas Mawr, Aberconwy House and Bodnant Garden, chapter 8 for the bridges and chapter 10 for Butterfly House.)

CRICCIETH
Early closing Wednesday.

Criccieth is a seaside resort of the pleasantly old-fashioned kind that relies on a sandy beach, small hotels and modest amusements to draw visitors. Like Barmouth, it grew up with the arrival of the Cambrian Coast railway, and its centre, the Green, is a typical Victorian feature. However, the castle, on its promontory by the shore, is an inescapable reminder that the town has a much older history and became a borough in the thirteenth century. The restored medieval church is worth visiting. The popular Black Rock Sands can be reached by walking to the east, while westwards there is a good path to Lloyd George's village of Llanystumdwy. (See chapter 4 for the castle and chapter 7 for the Lloyd George Museum.)

DINAS MAWDDWY

This former mining community lies beside the river Dyfi on the A470, 10 miles (16 km) east of Dolgellau, dominated on all sides by hills. It has retained much of its industrial character, although nowadays it is a popular holiday place. Its principal attraction is the Meirion Mill, set up to replace the declining slate industry. At the entrance to the mill there still stands the terminus of a railway built to carry slates down the valley to the main line at Cemmaes Road, and nearby is the historic packhorse bridge built by a rector of the parish in 1635. The minor road from here to lake Vyrnwy provides a dramatic drive over Bwlch-y-groes, passing through completely empty moorland. (See chapter 10 for Meirion Mill.)

DOLGELLAU
Early closing Wednesday; market day Friday.

At the meeting point of several roads and rivers, Dolgellau was bound to become important. It was formerly the county town of

Meirionnydd and still remains a busy commercial and administrative centre. It makes no brash attempt to attract visitors, but its impressive bridge, its dark stone and slate buildings and its irregular streets winding away from a central square have their own fascination and are certainly in keeping with its splendid position beneath Cadair Idris. Enthusiasts for architecture will appreciate the informative town trail and should not miss the mainly eighteenth-century church. The nearby Precipice Walk and Torrent Walk have long been famous. (See chapter 4 for Cymer Abbey, chapter 5 for Brithdir church and chapter 11 for Cadair Idris.)

FFESTINIOG

This is an unremarkable village to the south of Blaenau Ffestiniog. There is a pleasant walk to the south from the former station (OS 124: SH 704418) to the waterfall known as Rhaeadr Cynfal.

HARLECH
Early closing Wednesday.

This small and unassuming place grew up around Edward I's castle, and its main function today is to cater for the thousands of visitors each year who come to visit the spectacular site and also to enjoy the nearby holiday beaches and hill walks. (See chapter 4 for the castle, chapter 7 for the Chwarel Hen slate caverns and chapter 3 for nearby prehistoric sites.)

The market house, Dolgellau.

HOLYHEAD

Selected at the turn of the eighteenth century as the site of an Irish ferry port, Holyhead became the objective of Thomas Telford's famous road which, as the A5, still runs largely over the same route for a distance of nearly 270

Left: *The former terminus of the railway to Cemmaes Road, Dinas Mawddwy.*
Right: *The packhorse bridge at Dinas Mawddwy.*

The Two Kings sculpture by the sea at Harlech.

miles (434 km) from London. The town stands on Holy Island, which was precariously linked to Anglesey until Telford built his massive Stanley Embankment. Apart from the interest of the port itself, there is a good deal of nautical activity along the waterfront between the old and new harbours. Holyhead also has the surviving walls of the Roman fort of Caer Gybi, within which stands the church, which has stained glass by William Morris and Edward Burne-Jones. The town is over-shadowed by Holyhead Mountain, excellent for walking and for viewing some of the many prehistoric sites in the area, and there are good beaches at Trearddur to the south. The short crossing time of three and a half hours makes a day trip to the Irish port of Dun Laoghaire an attractive possibility. (See chapter 3 for the Roman fort and prehistoric sites, chapter 5 for the church, chapter 7 for the maritime museum and chapter 8 for industrial archaeology.)

LLANBERIS

Although a tourist honeypot in the summer holiday season (in addition to its other attractions it is at the foot of the dramatic Llanberis pass), Llanberis is a focal point of interest for the visitor. Like Betws-y-coed, it developed in Victorian times as a centre for climbing, walking and sightseeing, and it has enlarged its appeal to tourists ever since. The village stands near the point where Llyn Padarn and Llyn Peris (once a single lake) are separated by a narrow stretch of dry land. The whole area of Llyn Padarn is now a country park, with a lakeside narrow-gauge railway and enjoyable walks. The spectacular Dinorwic slate quarries across the lake are now the site of a museum, and a well concealed power station (hydro-electric pumped storage) has been constructed nearby on Llyn Peris. Llanberis is also the terminus of the Snowdon Mountain Railway. (See chapter 2 for Llyn Padarn Country Park, chapter 4 for Dolbadarn Castle, chapter 6 for Bryn Bras Castle, chapter 7 for the Welsh Slate Museum and The Power of Wales, and chapter 9 for Llanberis Lake Railway and Snowdon Mountain Railway.)

LLANDEGAI

The village lies at the south gates of Penrhyn Castle, 2 miles (3 km) south-east of Bangor, and is a notable example of a nineteenth-century estate village. The church contains interesting tombs and memorials. (See chapter 6 for Penrhyn Castle.)

LLANDUDNO

Early closing (winter) Wednesday.

Llandudno is Gwynedd's largest and most sophisticated seaside resort, with luxury hotels, a lively night life and a whole range of entertainments. At the same time it is recognised as one of Britain's finest Victorian towns, having been purpose-built from the nineteenth century onwards by the local landowners, the Mostyns. Early settlement here centred on the massive headland known as the Great Orme, where there are still prehistoric survivals, and copper was mined here in the eighteenth and early nineteenth centuries. The opening of the Chester-Holyhead railway in the 1840s was the incentive for turning a small mining village into a major resort. The new town was planned on a grand scale, with a long promenade following the curve of the northern beach and a second major thoroughfare, Mostyn Street, running parallel behind it. A third principal road, Gloddaeth Street, connects the northern beach with the western shore facing Conwy Bay. The grid pattern of subsidiary roads was planned with meticulous care, and strict regulations governed the size of buildings. Later development has not spoilt the harmony and spaciousness of the original concept.

As a result the town has a double appeal – as an exhibition of Victorian architecture, interesting if not distinguished, and as a resort offering a wide range of recreation. Many of its older attractions have been retained, for example the splendid pier with sailings to the Isle of Man, the 'Happy Valley' gardens and the tramway to the summit of the Great Orme (a cable-car service also operates), which is now a country park, offering exhilarating walks and fine views (see chapter 2). A toll road circumnavigates the headland. Newer facilities include the Canolfan Aberconwy conference and leisure centre, three golf courses and a heated swimming pool.

The vast north beach remains the principal attraction, although the less sheltered and less developed west shore has its devotees. The claim that Charles Dodgson (Lewis Carroll) was inspired to write *Alice's Adventures in Wonderland* while exploring the west shore with Alice Liddell and her family is open to doubt, but there is nevertheless a White Rabbit Memorial here.

The neighbouring small resort of **Deganwy**, between Llandudno and Conwy, has the traces of a castle which played a great part in resisting the Norman advance into Gwynedd. Another enjoyable excursion from Llandudno is the very scenic trip on British Rail's Conwy Valley line to Blaenau Ffestiniog. (See chapter 7 for the art gallery.)

LLANERCHYMEDD

This large village was for long the market centre of northern Anglesey, specialising in boot and shoe production, and it still has a small-town atmosphere. A lane from here leads to a parking place beside Llyn Alaw (see chapter 2).

LLANFAIRFECHAN

Llanfairfechan is a small resort of considerable charm to the west of Conwy. Good early twentieth-century architecture, much of it by a local architect, Herbert North, is combined with a pleasant beach, and the locally available 'history trail' is a guide to a fascinating walk through the area's prehistory. There are longer rambles into the hills above.

LLANFAIRPWLLGWYNGYLL

This Anglesey village became famous for the Victorian publicity stunt which gave it the much lengthened name seen at the old railway station and elsewhere. In practice the name is reduced to Llanfairpwll or Llanfair PG. It was a toll point on the Holyhead road, and one of Thomas Telford's distinctive tollhouses survives complete with its table of rates. Also of interest is the Marquess of Anglesey's Column, erected in memory of the first Marquess's gallantry at Waterloo. Its spiral staircase (115 steps) can be climbed to reach a platform with magnificent views. (See chapter 3 for local prehistoric sites, chapter 6 for Plas Newydd and chapter 10 for Anglesey Sea Zoo and Anglesey Bird World.)

The Great Orme, which shelters the resort of Llandudno.

CHAPTER 12

LLANGEFNI
The former county town of Anglesey, Llangefni is still its commercial and agricultural centre. There is an unusual church of 1824. (See chapter 10 for Hen Blas.)

LLANRWST
Early closing Thursday; market day Tuesday.
The 'capital' of the Conwy valley, Llanrwst is a small bustling town with a famous seventeenth-century bridge traditionally attributed to Inigo Jones. On the western side of the bridge is Tu-hwnt-i'r-bont, a rare local example of a fifteenth-century building (National Trust). (See chapter 5 for the church, Gwydir Uchaf Chapel and Llanrhychwyn church, chapter 6 for Gwydir Castle and chapter 10 for Trefriw Wells Spa and Trefriw Woollen Mills.)

LLANYSTUMDWY
This village to the west of Criccieth is closely associated with the former Prime Minister David Lloyd George, who is the subject of a small museum (see chapter 7). A 'heritage trail' is available, pointing out local buildings and features with Lloyd George connections, including his early home, his grave and his memorial by Sir Clough Williams-Ellis. There is a good walk from here by the river northwards up the Dwyfach valley and another along the coast to Criccieth.

MAENTWROG
The attractive nineteenth-century village takes its name from the large stone – *maen twrog* – in the churchyard and was established as the estate village of William Oakley, whose former mansion, Tan-y-Bwlch, can be seen in the trees across the valley. (The house is now the National Park residential study centre.) The church, altered in 1896, contains some fine craftsmanship.

MENAI BRIDGE
This is the little Anglesey town that grew up from the 1820s around the western side of Thomas Telford's suspension bridge. It was in the parish of Llandysilio, and the original church on its near-island site can be reached by following the Belgian Promenade from the bridge. The tiny church is rather overshadowed by its churchyard and the mound carrying a war memorial. There is an excellent view of the Britannia Bridge from here. (See chapter 8 for the road and rail bridges and chapter 10 for the Butterfly Palace.)

MOELFRE
This is another of the small harbour villages that are such a feature of the north Anglesey coast. It is a centre for cliff walking, both on its own headland and along the coast to east and west.

Porthmadog harbour.

NEFYN

Nefyn and its neighbour Morfa Nefyn make up a small but popular seaside resort on the north Lleyn coast. The long straight road that crosses the Lleyn peninsula from Pwllheli to Morfa Nefyn was created as part of a project to site an Irish ferry port at nearby Porth Dinllaen (see Porthmadog). Porth Dinllaen, however, has remained an idyllic group of beach-side cottages. (See chapter 5 for Pistyll church and chapter 7 for the maritime museum.)

PENMAENMAWR

This small seaside resort gained a good deal of prestige in the late nineteenth century as one of the favourite watering-places of William Gladstone, although it was also a busy port for the shipment of stone (the quarrying activity has cut away much of the headland). It was notorious, too, as one of the most dangerous places on the northern coast road, since the road had to be taken in perilous fashion round the edge of the headland above seas that were frequently rough. There was significant pre-historic activity in the area, and a locally available 'history trail' guides visitors to the main sites, providing good walking in the process.

PORTHMADOG

Early closing Wednesday; market day (summer) Friday.

The town was largely the creation of William Madocks (1773-1828), a zealous improver who bought land here in 1797 and conceived several large-scale projects. One was for an Irish ferry port at Porth Dinnllaen, near Nefyn on the Lleyn peninsula, and the new town of Tremadog (see separate entry) was built as a staging post on the road to it. Another was the reclamation of the vast waste of Traeth Mawr, to be achieved by holding back the sea behind an embankment across the estuary. Although the results were never satisfactory, the project did provide a site for Porthmadog, and the long embankment (the Cob) now carries the main road, a footpath and the narrow-gauge line south-east of Porthmadog. Porthmadog harbour, formed artificially by river diversions, also resulted from Madocks's vision, providing a much needed outlet for the slates from Blaenau Ffestiniog, which were transported to the quays on a new tramway (later the Ffestiniog

Railway). Porthmadog's long main street is now a major local shopping centre and very crowded in the summer season. (See chapter 7 for the maritime museum and chapter 9 for the Ffestiniog and Welsh Highland Railways.)

PORTMEIRION

(See entry in chapter 10.)

PWLLHELI

Early closing Thursday; market day Wednesday.

In recent years Pwllheli has become almost synonymous with the big holiday camp (open to day visitors) which occupies its own site well to the east, but the old town has for long been the shopping and commercial centre for the Lleyn peninsula, and the area to the north of the railway has some handsome Victorian architecture and homely streets. The holiday area is South Beach, close to the harbour, which was once a thriving commercial port and is now much used by pleasure craft. (See chapter 5 for St Cybi's Well at Llangybi and chapter 6 for Pennarth Fawr medieval house, Plas Glyn-y-Weddw and Plas-yn-Rhiw.)

TREMADOG

See under Porthmadog, above, for the background to this neat planned town, developed on reclaimed land in the very early nineteenth century. Its centre is a small square containing a hotel and the market hall, which once also served as the social centre with a theatre and ballroom, and there is a notable nonconformist chapel of the same period. T. E. Lawrence (Lawrence of Arabia) was born here.

TYWYN

Tywyn is best known today for its popular beaches, but the town centre is some distance away from them. It owes its resort character to John Corbett of Droitwich in Worcestershire who bought the land in the 1870s and set out to create a watering-place. Several buildings, including the Corbett Arms and the Assembly Rooms, recall that period. The big church received a substantial restoration at the same time, but it contains a stone bearing what are believed to be the first written words in Welsh. (See chapter 4 for Castell y Bere and chapter 9 for the Talyllyn Railway and narrow-gauge museum.)

Ffestiniog power station.

13
Itineraries for motorists

1. Anglesey (north). Menai Bridge – A545 – Beaumaris – minor roads to Penmon (Priory) – Llanddona – Pentraeth – A5025 – Llanallgo – Amlwch (Parys Mountain) – Cemaes (Cemlyn Bay) – Llanfaethlu – Llanfachraeth – B5109 – Llangefni – Menai Bridge.

2. Anglesey (south). Menai Bridge – Llanfairpwll – A4080 – Brynsiencyn (prehistoric sites) – Newborough (Newborough Warren) – Malltraeth – Aberffraw – Llanfaelog – A5 – Holyhead (Mountain and South Stack) – B4545 – Trearddur – A5 – Gwalchmai – Menai Bridge.

3. Lleyn peninsula. Criccieth – A497 – Llanystumdwy – Pwllheli – Llanbedrog – Abersoch – B4413 – Botwnnog – Aberdaron – Pen-y-groeslon – B4417 – Tudweiliog – Nefyn – Llanaelhaearn – A499 – Clynnog Fawr – minor road – Pen-y-groes – A487, then B4411 – Criccieth.

4. Northern Snowdonia. Bangor – Conwy – Trefriw – Llanrwst – Betws-y-coed – Capel Curig – Nant Ffrancon pass – Bethesda – Bangor.

5. Central Snowdonia. Caernarfon – Llanberis – Llanberis pass – Pen-y-pass – A498 – Nantgwynant pass – Beddgelert – Tremadoc – Porthmadog – Pen-y-groes – Caernarfon.

6. Southern Snowdonia. Porthmadog – A487 – Maentwrog – A496 – Blaenau Ffestiniog – Ffestiniog – Bala – A494 – Dolgellau – A487 – Corris – A493 – Aberdyfi – Tywyn – Dolgellau – A496 – Barmouth – Harlech – Porthmadog.

14
Tourist information centres

Those marked with an asterisk (*) are open in the summer only.

Aberdyfi: *The Wharf, Aberdyfi LL35 0EO. Telephone: 0654 72321.
Abersoch: *The Village Hall, Abersoch. Telephone: 075881 2929.
Bala: *High Street, Bala LL23 7AB. Telephone: 0678 520367.
Bangor: *Theatr Gwynedd, Deiniol Road, Bangor LL57 2TL. Telephone: 0248 352786.
Barmouth: *The Old Library, Barmouth LL42 1LU. Telephone: 0341 280787.
Beddgelert: Llewelyn Cottage, Beddgelert LL55 4YA. Telephone: 076686 293.
Betws-y-coed: *Royal Oak Stables, Betws-y-coed LL24 0AH. Telephone: 06902 426 or 665.
Blaenau Ffestiniog: *High Street, Blaenau Ffestiniog LL41 3HD. Telephone: 0766 830360.
Caernarfon: Oriel Pendeitsh, Caernarfon LL55 2PB. Telephone: 0286 672232.
Conwy: *Conwy Castle Visitor Centre, Conwy. Telephone: 0492 592248.
Corris: *Craft Centre, Corris SY20 9RF. Telephone: 065473 244.
Criccieth: *The Sweet Shop, 47 High Street, Criccieth LL52 0EY. Telephone: 0766 523303.
Dolgellau: *The Bridge, Dolgellau LL40 1LF. Telephone: 0341 422888.
Harlech: *High Street, Harlech LL46 2YA. Telephone: 0766 780658.
Holyhead: Marine Square, Salt Island Approach, Holyhead LL65 1DR. Telephone: 0407 2622.
Llanberis: *Amgueddfa'r Gogledd / Museum of the North, Llanberis LL55 4UR. Telephone: 0286 870765.
Llandudno: Chapel Street, Llandudno LL30 2YU. Telephone: 0492 76413.
Llanfairpwllgwyngyll: Station Site, Llanfairpwllgwyngyll LL61 5UJ. Telephone: 0248 713177.
Porthmadog: High Street, Porthmadog LL49 9LP. Telephone: 0766 512981.
Pwllheli: Y Maes, Pwllheli LL53 6HE. Telephone: 075861 3000.
Tywyn: High Street, Tywyn LL36 9AD. Telephone: 0654 710070

Corris Craft Centre houses one of Gwynedd's tourist information centres.

Wylfa Nuclear Power Station
Bull Bay
Cemaes
AMLWCH
Llan
Llanrhwydrys
Cemlyn Bay
Parys Mountain
Porth Swtan
Llanbabo
Porth Trwyn
Llanddeusant
Din Lli
Porth Trefadog
Porth
Llyn Alaw
North Stack
Tywyn-mawr
Llanerchymedd
Myn
Caer-y-Twr
HOLYHEAD
Bod
South Stack
Penrhos
Presaddfed
Ty Mawr hut circles
Stanley
burial chambers
Embankment
ANGLESEY
Trearddur
HOLY ISLAND
LLANGEFNI
Rhoscolyn
Rhosneigr
Hen Bla
Llangadwaladr
Barclodiad-y-Gawres
Malltraeth
Porth Trecastell
Bodo
Aberffraw
Castell Bryn Gwyn
Newborough
Bird World
Newborough Forest
Llanddwyn Island
CAERNARFO

Air World
Dinas Dinlle
Llan
Parc Glynllifon

Llan
Clynnog Faw

Trefor
Tre'r Ceiri hillfort

Porth Dinllaen
Pistyll
Llangyt
Morfa Nefyn
Nefyn
Llanystumd
LLEYN PENINSULA
Penarth Fawr
PWLLHELI

Traeth Penllech
Llangwnnadl
Plas Glyn-y-Weddw
Porth Iago
Porth Oer
Plas-yn- Porth
Rhiw Neigwl
Aberdaron
Abersoch
Braich y Pwll
Creigiau Llanengan
Porth Gwineu
Ysgo
Porth Ceiriad

Bardsey Island

KEY

✳ Coast and countryside (Ch. 2)
⊓ Site of archaeological interest (Ch. 3)
C Castle (Ch. 4)
▲ Monastic building (Ch. 4)
+ Church or chapel (Ch. 5)
▲ House or garden (Ch. 6)
M Museum (Ch. 7)
I Industrial archaeology (Ch. 8)
+--+ Railway (British Rail) (Ch. 9)
⊥⊥⊥ Railway (narrow-gauge) (Ch. 9)
O Other attraction (Ch. 10)
△ Mountain (Ch. 11)
■ Town or village (Ch. 12)
● Other places

GWYNEDD

Index

Page numbers in italic refer to illustrations.